TRAVELLERS
IN
Arabia
BRITISH EXPLORERS IN SAUDI ARABIA

Edited by **Eid Al Yahya**

IN MEMORY OF ST JOHN ARMITAGE *

No, don't mock me for sobbing
or for weeping waterfalls over a single grave
in England.

Let me.
Sentiments evoke sentiments.
All graves are St John's grave.

Eid Al Yahya
LONDON 14 MARCH 2005

* St John Armitage, who rigorously checked, with numerous suggestions, the material presented in the body of this book, died on October 19th, 2004. He unfortunately never had the chance to see this work appear in published form. He will be remembered by all who knew and worked with him for, amongst other things, his passionate interest in Arabian history.   E.Y.

Introduction

This book presents Arabia between the 1860s and 1950s as seen through the eyes of some of the most notable British travellers to Saudi Arabia, including such well-known figures as H. St J. B. Philby and Sir Wilfred Thesiger. The striking pictures and detailed accounts of their travels contribute greatly to our knowledge of the history of Saudi Arabia and Saudi-British relations.

The conditions of desert travel and the towns and tribes of Arabia were brought vividly to life in the works of Victorian travellers such as Doughty and Palgrave, and in the journals, books and diaries of those who followed. Lady Anne Blunt's sketches and delicate watercolours were forerunners of the thousands of photographs taken by her successors, whose cameras captured the people and scenery of their day.

Among them was Captain Shakespear, who, as Political Agent in Kuwait, took the earliest known photograph of Ibn Saud, the future king of Saudi Arabia. Colonel Leachman took the first photographs of Riyadh two years later, and in 1914 Gertrude Bell took some of the earliest and best photographs of Hail, that isolated stronghold on the southern fringe of the Nafud desert. T.E. Lawrence captured scenes of the Arab Revolt during World War One, and Bertram Thomas took the first photographs of the Rub' Al-Khali or Empty Quarter, the great southern desert of Arabia. Philby and Thesiger made a major contribution to the pictorial archive of the desert and the town, and the Riyadh photographs taken by de Gaury and Rendel show the impressive desert capital – described by Philby as 'Queen of the Desert' – as it was between the two world wars, with its battlemented walls and bustling streets.

The travellers went to Arabia for a variety of reasons: to discover a city "more wondrous" than Petra, to fill in the blanks on the maps of the day, or as emissaries on political and military missions. Only Palgrave travelled in disguise, adopting an Arab identity. For almost all the others, Arab dress was the order of the day, although Shakespear wore his uniform throughout, occasionally with Arab head-dress and cloak. For the most part they travelled under the protection of either tribes or government – sometimes both – and their accounts pay tribute to the hospitality and companionship they encountered on their journeys.

All these pioneers faced the hazards of desert travel in varying degrees: the fierce heat of the day, the freezing cold of night. Many experienced hunger and thirst, exhaustion and illness. It is tempting to ask why they endured these hardships. Perhaps the answer lies, for some, in Thesiger's words: "This cruel land can cast a spell which no temperate clime can reach."

E.Y.

King Abdul-Aziz

Through the eyes of the travellers

King Abdul-Aziz bin Abdul-Rahman bin Feisal Al Saud, commonly known as Ibn Saud, was the towering figure of modern Arabian history. As Sultan of Nejd from 1926, and thereafter King of Saudi Arabia, it was to him that many of the travellers featured in this exhibition came to pay their respects – indeed, it is Ibn Saud who provides one of the strongest threads through the journeys recorded in the photographs that follow.

A close friend of Captain Shakespear and H. St J. B. Philby, admired by Colonel Leachman, Gertrude Bell, Gerald de Gaury and Sir George Rendel, King Abdul-Aziz made a strong impression on all who met him.

Here is Captain Shakespear, writing in 1910:
> "Abdul-Aziz, now in his 31st year, is fair, handsome and considerably above average Arab height. He is a broad-minded and generous man who does not descend to mean actions."

Six years later, Gertrude Bell met Ibn Saud in Basra:
> "We had an extraordinarily interesting day with Ibn Saud, who is one of the most striking personalities I have encountered. He is splendid to look at, well over 6'3", with an immense amount of dignity and self-possession. As a leader of irregular forces he is of proved daring and he combines with his qualities as a soldier that grasp of statecraft which is yet more highly prized."

In 1935, Gerald de Gaury recorded that:
> "He speaks forcibly and well, decorating his conversation with old Arab proverbs, Bedouin sayings and quotations from the Koran. When he is speaking on diplomatic and political business he generally speaks at considerable length, arranging his facts to be noted by the listener in the clearest way, point by point to the climax, whereupon he leans back, shifts his position somewhat, and smiles with appealing charm."

The legacy

King Abdul-Aziz was born in 1876 or 1880 and raised in Kuwait, where his family lived in exile. In 1901 he selected 60 companions and headed for the Al Saud stronghold of Riyadh, which at the time was held by the Turkish-backed Rashid tribe. Early one January morning in 1902, Abdul-Aziz and a small group of his finest men climbed onto the rooftops of a house adjoining that of the Rashidi governor. Together with a reserve force waiting below, they ambushed the fortress and overwhelmed the guards. That very morning, the people of Riyadh were proclaiming the return of the Al Saud.

Thereafter, Abdul-Aziz spread religious reform and Saudi power through a mixture of military conquest and tough political negotiation. By 1926 he had united the Holy Cities of Mecca and Medina and the Red Sea coastal province of Hejaz. In 1932 he renamed his kingdom Saudi Arabia, and slowly began to introduce the innovations he knew were vital to the future of his country: the telephone, motor transport and wireless telegraphy.

The discovery of oil in his kingdom was to present Abdul-Aziz with fresh challenges; by the time the 'fifty-fifty' arrangement with the Arabian-American Oil Company (Aramco) had been negotiated in 1951, Saudi Arabia was a very different country from the poor, sparse land which he had captured a few decades earlier.

Perhaps the greatest legacy that King Abdul-Aziz left to his people was internal security. Until his reign, towns were walled, gates were barred at nightfall and all desert journeys were undertaken at risk from raiders or feuding tribes. In the unified Kingdom of Saudi Arabia, such defences became increasingly unnecessary. King Abdul-Aziz travelled widely and frequently among the tribes of his kingdom, cementing loyalties as he went. By the time of his death in 1953, a new generation of travellers could camp at nightfall without fear of attack. This ambitious, determined, tough-minded ruler had laid the foundations of the modern Kingdom of Saudi Arabia.

The final word on King Abdul-Aziz should perhaps go to the Englishman who knew him best, Abdullah Philby, who wrote:
> "He achieved greatness by his own merit and by virtue of a strong personality, which is almost without parallel in the history of the Arabs."

Above:
H.M. King Abdul-Aziz meets Prime Minister Winston Churchill on the terrace
of the Auberge du Lac Hotel, Egypt, 17 February 1945.

The Contributors

S o much has been written on the first British travellers who ventured into Arabia that this great theme calls for some distillation. The three short essays gathered in this chapter, each written by a prominent hsitorian of Arabia, provide an introduction to the subject, presenting the various travellers in their historical context with both breadth and concision.

British Travellers in Arabia: From Pilgrim to Tourist

H. St J. B. Armitage C.B.E.

The material presented in this book covers one hundred years of the three and a quarter centuries since the first recorded British traveller to what Saudi Arabia is today.

There were many other British travellers who might have been included in this collection some of whom I will cover here. But I should also mention that exploration of Saudi Arabia was not a British prerogative. To name but a few other westerners, Burckhardt, the Swiss, in 1812, Wallin, the Swede in 1845 and 1848, Musil, the Czech, and Raunkier, the Dane, both pre-WWI, were amongst those who set both example and challenge to the British.

How many of those who travel in the Rub' al Khali – the Empty Quarter – today realise that crossing it was once the final and greatest prize of Arabian Exploration left to the western traveller? Many had dreamed of it, but none attempted it until Bertram Thomas succeeded in crossing from Dhufar to Qatar in 1931 much to the disappointment of Abdullah Philby, his one time master in Transjordan, whose planned crossing had been frustrated on three occasions.

Thirteen years earlier in 1918, Philby had been unable to go beyond the limits to his travels along the desert's northern boundary as prescribed by Ibn Saud and so had to return to Riyadh 'content with what had been achieved and the hope of satisfying some day the insatiable craving within me to penetrate the recesses of that Empty Quarter.' His plan to make the crossing in 1924 was thwarted by illness and preparations for a crossing in 1931, which would have coincided with Thomas's journey, had to be postponed until the beginning of 1932. Philby conceded the honours of priority to Thomas in a mixture of metaphors,

'...As the Arab poet sang of old:
T 'was I that learned him in the archer's art
At me, his hand grown strong, he launched his dart...'

And, acknowledging the remaining challenge:

He had won the race, and it only remained for me to finish the course.'

That task – his 1932 crossing and other exploratory journeys – engaged him for twenty more years by which time, 1951, Wilfred Thesiger had established himself – in Philby's words ' – *as second to none in the long line and honourable role of Arabian explorers.'* Philby wrote that by then, the mid-twentieth century, the mainstream of Arabian exploration *'may be regarded as having come to an end…but there are many creeks and backwaters still awaiting the attention of explorers yet to come…'*

Thomas, Philby and Thesiger were the last of the true explorers, but what of the British who preceded them?

The first account we have is that of Joseph Pitts, a cabin boy who had been captured by Algerian pirates in 1678, sold into slavery and forced to apostatise. In 1680, making the pilgrimage with his master, he was the first Englishman to visit Mecca and Madinah. He was later manumitted, returning to England in 1693.

Pitts was followed in the eighteenth century by a number of maritime visitors to the Hijaz ports, but it was over a hundred years later before the next known British visitor to Madina when, for a brief period in 1812, Thomas Keith, a Scotsman, had been Governor of that city. Whilst serving with the 78th Highlanders in Egypt he had been captured, chosen to convert to Islam and he had entered the service of Muhammad Ali, the Viceroy of Egypt. In 1815 he was killed in a clash with the forces of Abdullah bin Saud.

Seven years later, in 1819, came the historic crossing of the Peninsula from Qatif to Yanbu' by Captain G.F. Sadlier, the first by a westerner, an achievement unequalled until Captain W.H.I. Shakespear's crossing from Kuwait via Riyadh to Egypt in 1914.

Sadlier had been sent by the Governor General of India to meet Ibrahim Pasha of Egypt who was campaigning against the Al Saud in Najd. He travelled under the tribal protection of the Bani Khalid from Qatif to al Hasa where he learned that the Pasha, having destroyed the Wahhabi capital of Dara'iyyah after an eight months siege, was already withdrawing towards the Hijaz. Although it was open to him to return to India he decided to continue with his mission. Under Turkish protection, he followed the Pasha's trail from Dara'iyyah through *'a desert county…now rendered a waste by the destruction and devastations of war'* to Anaiza, Rass and Hanakiyya before reaching Bin Ali on the outskirts of Madina where he finally met with the Pasha. He then continued on the coast reaching Yanbu eighty-four days after leaving Qatif.

After Sadlier, Captain Richard Burton, translator-to-be of the *Arabian Nights*, made the pilgrimage in 1853, but that famous adventure was not to be, as he had hoped, the springboard *'for the purpose of removing that opprobrium of modern adventure, the huge white blot which in our maps still notes the Eastern and Central regions of Arabia'* – the Rub' al Khali – either by crossing from Medina to Musqat, or from Mecca to Mukalla. His pilgrimage to the Holy Cities – where other Europeans had preceded him and whose accounts he commended – was of less importance geographically than his two later expeditions to the land of Midian (North–West Hijaz) in 1877-78. There he had discovered the sites of some thirty-one ruined cities, but not the gold he was seeking.

Later British pilgrims, whose accounts of the Holy Cities would complement Burton's study, were J.F. Keane in 1887, A.J.B. Wavell, (cousin of Field Marshall Lord Wavell) in 1908-09 and Eldon Rutter in 1925-26. Wavell travelled third class by the Hijaz Railway from Damascus for £3.10 shillings! Rutter landed in Asir from Massowa and rode to Mecca on a camel up the coastal track to Al Lith, and thence via Wadi Yalamlam to Mecca. The account of his pilgrimage and the twelve months he spent in the Hijaz is a classic study that gives a clearer impression of life and custom in the Holy Cities than Burton's scholarly work. He was to participate in the first Pilgrimage under the authority of Ibn Saud. Both he and Wavell travelled openly as British Muslims as would do Lord Headley in 1924 and lady Evelyn Cobbold in 1933. It is believed that the first to do so was Hermann Bicknell in 1862.

(Incidentally the British minister was to report, rather unkindly I feel, of Lady Cobbold's pilgrimage *She was allowed to go to the Holy Cities on the strength of having embraced Islam nearly 60 years before, although in the interval she had had less practical experience of the faith than of the duties of an English wife and mother and the pleasures of a great lady.'*)

In 1862, Bicknell's year, William Gifford Palgrave, who had taken holy orders, was commissioned by Napoleon III to report on Hail and Riyadh. He travelled as a Christian Arab together with a Greek priest, both under assumed Arab names. They followed the route from Ma'an to Jauff where they stayed for two weeks, then through the Nafud at the height of summer, to Hail. In October they arrived in Riyadh, which had emerged as the capital of Najd, the first Europeans to enter the city. After five uncomfortable weeks there, Palgrave and his companion, fearing for their lives, took an opportunity to leave quietly for Hufuf and Qatif from where they crossed to Bahrain on Christmas Eve. Philby, amongst others, cast strong doubts on parts of Palgrave's account, but despite those doubts and Palgrave's own admission of hearsay as the basis for some of his book, he holds his place in the story of Arabian exploration. Palgrave himself wrote that the main object of the research was *'the men of the land, rather than the land of the men.'* A fair assessment might be that of the late Dr. Robin Bidwell, who wrote in his account of travellers in Arabia that *'Palgrave was less interested in solid facts than in conveying impression and in this, right or wrong, he usually succeeded.'*

The first official contact between the British and the ruling family of Al Saud occurred in the early spring of 1865 when Lieutenant Colonel Lewis Pelly, the British Resident in Bushire, visited Imam Faisal ibn Saud only a few months before the latter's death. Pelly's dispatch to the Government of Bombay describes in detail his meetings with the Imam Faisal, the Court and its members and his return march to the coast at Qatif. The appendices cover a wide range of subjects including geological and botanical notes, route reports, breeds of horses, currency and weights and measures. Pelly also established the longitude and latitude of Riyadh for the first time. Later in the year he gave an account of his visit to a meeting at the Royal Geographical Society at which Palgrave expressed the hope that *'others of the British service will follow in the same track, and complete the task of investigation.'* Almost fifty years were to pass before that hope was partially fulfilled, when Leachman – of whom I will speak later – reached Riyadh.

Today ninety years on *'others of the British service'* and their compatriots are still searching the highways and byways of Saudi Arabia. Eleven years after Pelly, Charles Doughty described by Philby before the advent of Thesiger, as the greatest of all the *"Arabians"*, was to begin the classic journey of Arabian exploration. Leaving Damascus with the Syrian Haj caravan of 1876, Doughty travelled down with it to Medain Salith, where he spent three months studying the baduin and collecting tomb inscriptions. He intended to return to Damascus with the returning caravan, but attracted to the wilderness and the people, he decided to travel further afield. For nearly two more years, nearly always on sufferance and often in danger, he travelled to Hail, Khaibar, Anazia and Buraida suffering many indignities and much hardship. Finally under the protection of Zamil, the governor of Buraida, and befriended by two families in Buraida, Kanneyni and the Bassams, he was able to join the famous annual *'Butter Caravan'* bound for Mecca, his friends arranging for him to leave during the last stage and travel via Taif down to Jedda where he embarked for Bombay. It was another ten years before *Arabia Deserta*, the account of his Arabian years, was published. Thirty more were to pass before it received the recognition it deserved and was published with a foreword by Lawrence of Arabia, who thought it was *'the first and indispensable work on Arabs of the desert.'*

Early in December 1878, a few months after Dougherty's departure from Jedda. Wilfred and Lady Anne Blunt, travelling openly as Europeans, left Damascus heading for Hail to visit Rashidi Amir's horse stud, which was famous throughout Arabia. They reached Jauf in early January two days after they had been attacked and robbed by a party of Rulla baduin, but after this initial misunderstanding the Rualla returned the Blunts' possessions, and became their guests! They then went on to Hail where their hospitable reception was very different to the hostility encountered by Doughty nine months earlier. There they saw for the first time a telephone, of which they wrote *'One of those toys…. which were in fashion last year in Europe.'* After two weeks in Hail they joined a returning Persian Haj caravan and travelled with it to Najaf. The wealth of information in their account of their journey, and their notes on the physical geography were important contributions to western knowledge of north-east Arabia. After the accounts by the Blunt's and Doughty little new was to be added nor any major British contribution made for nearly thirty years.

The last known British visitor to the region was William Richard Williamson who, on conversion to Islam, took the name Abdullah Fadhil Williamson – Haji Williamson – and became a living legend in the Gulf during the first half of the 20th century. He had hunted whale in the Arctic and traded in the South Seas before he arrived in Arabia, where he was to live and trade with the tribes, and go pearling, and gun running in the gulf as well as accompany oil exploration teams. In 1896 he joined the Haj caravan from Kuwait and travelled to Medina and Mecca via Hail, but his biographer records (state, claim, suggest) that he was so overwhelmed by the Amir's hospitality and the religious fervour of the journey that '…he was blind to the features of this remote city … He was more keenly interested in Muslim observances than in topographical data.'

Early in the next century Archibald Forder, a lay Protestant reader, arrived in Jauff from Jerusalem with four cases of Bibles and the extraordinary aim of propagating Christianity. He spent a fortnight there in January 1901, coinciding with Ramadan, safe under the protection of Amir Jawhar who had been host to the Blunts. Like Doughty twenty years earlier, he made no secret of his faith and endured similar hardships and indignities albeit over a much shorter period. The first known photographs of the castles at Jauff and Ma'arid were those taken by Forder, but after leaving Jauff on his return journey most of the photographic plates were destroyed by his escort. He was followed by Captains Aylmer and Butler in 1908 who, on leave from East Africa decided to return to England via the gulf. Choosing to travel from Baghdad to Damascus via Jauff instead of the direct route they filled another blank spot on the map with their detailed observations. They returned to England with a series of photographs of Jauff and a present from the Amir: two pairs of Arabian Oryx horns.

The following year Douglas Carruthers was to travel in search of the Oryx in north-west Arabia between the Hijaz Railway, the Western Nafud and the wadi Sirhan. Although he put his knowledge of the desert to good use in map-making during World

War I it was not until 1934 that he published the story of his exploration. He then wrote, that "The inner deserts – the Tubaiq hills and the Western Nafud – are almost as inviolate as they were when I visited them, while the Shararat wilderness still lacks description." And so they remained until the advent of the Middle East Anti-Locust Unit, the forerunner of Desert Locust Control, during WWII, and the United States Geological Service in the fifties.

Fifty years after Palgrave Captain Gerard Leachman, already a hardened desert traveller, left Damascus on his journey to Riyadh. En route through Qasim, he offended the Amir at Ayrun by 'My refusal to tell him what my business with Ibn Saud, although I should have been puzzled to tell him this, as in truth I had none.' On his way he found that Ibn Saud had issued orders for his comfort at every town 'which greatly smoothed matters'. He was greeted on his arrival in Riyadh by Ibn Saud himself who 'regretted that he couldn't have offered any better quarters…Since his arrival Riyadh ten years ago, and he had no leisure to add to or improve his palace'. During his stay he took the first photographs of Riyadh. As Ibn Saud would not agree to his continuing exploration to Jabrin and the Empty Quarter he left for the coast. Failing to persuade the Turkish authorities in Hasa to allow him to journey further South he went to Uqair, from where he crossed over to Bahrain on Christmas Day. Ten years later, in 1923, Ibn Saud gave Major R.E. Cheesman, whom he had previously met at Uqair, permission to explore in Hasa 'to shoot birds and collect skins.' Thus Cheesman was the first westerner to penetrate the Jafura sands bordering the Empty Quarter and reach the 'lost' derelict Oasis of Jabrin.

But before Cheesman, four others were to make their mark in Arabian exploration and become legends in their lifetimes, and one of them well beyond his, they were Shakespear, Gertrude Bell, Philby and T.E. Lawrence.

Travelling down from Damascus early in 1914, Gertrude Bell was the second English lady to visit Hail where she was a virtual prisoner for the most of her brief stay before

continuing her journey to Baghdad. It had been in her mind to go further south, but failing to find an escort wrote, 'So Hayil must suffice for this year…I do not know what Ibn Saud is like…My next Arabian journey shall be to him.' It was not, for the rest of her life she was bound up with Iraq, but she did meet Ibn Saud when he visited Basra during the First World War.

Also in 1914 Captain Shakespear, the political agent in Kuwait, already well travelled in Kuwait and its borderlands, who gained the friendship of Ibn Saud since 1910 he had become the first Englishman to meet him, was given permission to undertake his long-planned journey across the Peninsula. He left Kuwait in February and five weeks later arrived in Riyadh (where he established his camp in the Shamsiya date grove, the heart of Riyadh to day) arriving there as Gertrude Bell was leaving Hail. From Riyadh he travelled for some days with Ibn Saud before leaving him near Haraimla to travel through Qasim and the Jebel Shammar to Jauf, the Sirhan and Aqaba then across the Sinai to Suez. In the course of his great expedition, which took four months Shakespear made eighty-seven camps. Eight months later on returning to Ibn Saud on a wartime mission he was killed in the battle at Jarrab between the forces of Ibn Saud and Ibn Rashid. The British who followed him on missions to Ibn Saud benefited from the latter's friendship for him, but none ever filled his place in the King's heart or mind.

Late in 1916, T.E. Lawrence, who was to become probably the best known of 'Arabians', arrived on the scene. It is his deeds rather than his travels, which have provided much of the impetus for to day's interest in the old Hijaz Railway although only three of his raids on the line were within Saudi Arabia's borders. More important geographically were his route records, particularly his south north route from the (travelogue, maps, descriptions) pf Carruthers and Bell. Neither the description of the Seven Pillars of Wisdom, nor the sketch map of his compass traverse over that sector during the course of his great ride from Wajh to Aqaba, fully reflect the geographical detail of his route notes, which helped fill one more blank in the geography of Arabia.

At the end of 1917 a third and more direct crossing than those of Sadlier and Shakespear was made by Philby who for ever after was to be connected with the history of Saudi Arabia. Sent by the Civil Commissioner in Mesopotamia, he arrived in Riyadh from Uqair, once leading port of entry for Najd, in November 1917, to succeed one Colonel Hamilton as head of the British Mission to Ibn Saud. The objectives of the mission were to tighten the blockade of supplies from Kuwait to the Rashidis in Hail and the Turkish garrison in Madina, and ensure that Ibn Saud's operations complimented, rather than conflicted with those of the Arab Revolt of King Hussain. He was to have joined by a British representative from Cairo, for discussions with Ibn Saud about the latter objective and to agree co-operation between him and King Hussain of Hijaz. As King Hussain refused to allow the Cairo representative to proceed from Jeddah on the grounds that the journey was too dangerous, Philby, with Ibn Saud's consent, travelled to Jeddah, thus proving the safety of the route if under Ibn Saud's protection. His journey from Uqair to Riyadh had taken ten days. His onward journey to Jeddah took another three weeks. He later wrote of Sadlier and Shakespear *'both my predecessors travelled throughout as British officers and gentlemen.'* Scorning (unlike Philby) the use of Arab garments and thus having, *'in the interests of their safety, to avoid contact with the Arabs on the way.'*

After his first steps in Arabia during those war years Philby was to continue his exploration until his last expeditions in the fifties. Between 1950 and 1953, he was to travel 3,000 miles in Midian – north-west Hejaz - and claim that he had seen more of that area than all his distinguished European predecessors put together. In 1951-52 he led an expedition with Belgium archaeologists, which in four months covered more than 5,000 kilometres in the border regions with Yemen.

Thesiger came onto the scene in the late forties and is best known for his crossing of the Rub' al-Khali and travels in the borderlands of Oman. But his first travels in Arabia south of Syria were in the north east of Saudi Arabia, and the latter must rank with his Rub' al-Khali crossings. He used motor transport in the north-east. But in the southwest his journeys along the Tihama and through the mountains of Asir and the southern Hejaz – more than 2,000 miles mainly on foot – were great pioneering achievements, which have not received the recognition they deserve.

Carruthers wrote of the earlier pioneers:

'These were my forerunners: and what a strange cavalcade they present! Of all nationalities, of every rank, of many trades: scientists, spies, Orientalists, adventurers, poets, Politicians! Types that seem to be attracted, for some curious reason, by desert Arabia.'

Looking back over the past century Carruthers' successors present an even stranger and more varied cavalcade. But in the creeks and backwaters of his and Philby's days are no more. Their details are set out in the route reports, which expatriate enthusiasts – the new pioneers – have so commendably produced for the guidance of their compatriots. Their followers – the travellers of today – are, perhaps, more tourists than explorers.

My travellers in Central Arabia and the Gulf

H.V.F. Winstone

Whenever I speak to Arab friends about 'my travellers' in their lands, even those who have read my books and are familiar with my version of events are liable to ask 'What were they actually doing? Why were these people travelling in hot, unfamiliar and hostile territories, enduring all sorts of privations and woes?' Of course, the question is usually rhetorical. I have a fairly good idea what is in their minds. The word that always comes to mind is Intelligence. In fact, that kind of 'intelligence', the peculiarly English kind, did sometimes come into it, but most of them were bent first and foremost on journeying into the unknown, on coming to terms with tribal life under conditions of extreme austerity, and of course filling in those white blots on the map as they used to say.

Whatever their motives, they were remarkable men and women – soldiers and politicals, wanderers and explorers. By and large, they inhabited the fringes of Britain's imperial story. I began to research their lives in the hope of building up a background story that would entice the publishing world. Some of the people I spoke to knew of Gertrude Bell, though most confused her with Vanessa Bell and the Bloomsbury set. None of my acquaintance had ever heard of Captain Shakespear or Gerard Leachman, and even people long since dead who had written about the latter thought his first name was Gerald. It was a fascinating untold story that gradually emerged from my very tentative studies. It became a personal adventure.

As most of you will know, it all started with Captain Shakespear. That first excursion into the 19th and early 20th century politics of central Arabia led in quick succession to Gertrude Bell, Leachman (I stole the title 'OC Desert' from a wartime article in *Blackwell's*), Parker Pasha, and on to Lady Anne Blunt and the archaeologists Leonard Woolley and Howard Carter.

It was an aged Kuwaiti who first set me on my journey of discovery. He was a wealthy man of the post-oil era when I met him; if I remember correctly a cigarette tycoon. He recalled to me the days of his youth in Kuwait when he fell victim to smallpox. It was I gathered about the year 1910. Like others who were stricken with infectious diseases in those days he was confined to a tent in the desert, hostage to fate, seldom visited by fellow humans. There were no medical treatments. But he was visited often by an Englishman who wandered in and out of the desert, usually on hunting trips, dressed as an officer of the Raj complete with topi, sometimes accompanied by tribal Shaikhs and by his own entourage of Indian servants, his faithful Arab jemader Khalaq, saluki dogs, and sinister hooded hawk by the name of Shalwa. And he always brought with him food and water for the invalid. The invalid eventually recovered and never forgot the benefactor who turned out to be HBM's Political Agent in Kuwait - Captain Skaishpear as they called him. As the story unfolded, it dawned on me that this was the man of whom Lawrence had written in the early chapters of *The Seven Pillars of Wisdom*, of whose 'magnificence' and splendid isolation the Arabs spoke in their camp fire conversations.

Gertrude Bell is the most significant – certainly in the topical sense – of my biographical subjects. She and her friends and enemies in Baghdad – and there were plenty of both – were after all in the front line of the first of the 20th century wars in Iraq that would become the blueprint of subsequent struggles which have time and again threatened the peace of the world. I have given the book a new introduction that I happily and proudly describe as one of barely concealed anger. More of Al Khatun, 'The Lady', in due course.

Shakespear was, and I suggest remains, the foremost among Englishmen in the territory of Al Saud. In any case, it is only natural that we have a bias towards our first born, and I am sure you will understand if I give him priority among Arabian explorers and political emissaries. Most importantly on this occasion, he was the one Englishman of his day whose unswerving support for the founding father of the Kingdom was to mark him out as a uniquely perceptive figure in an administration that was then as now decidedly equivocal in its Middle East policies.

From the moment of their first meeting, Shakespear became the avowed supporter of Bin Saud's claim to leadership of the Arabs of the Peninsula. 'He stands head and shoulders above all other Arab leaders' he wrote in one of his early reports to government. But though supported by his immediate chief Sir Percy Cox, he was for a good many years the lone protagonist. I am reminded of the words of Lord Crewe, Prime Minister Asquith's deputy, that the Foreign Office was terrified of the activities of Shakespear and Cox in the Persian Gulf and the territory that was then known in official parlance as 'Turkish Arabia'. It was also in connection with Shakespear that Crew reminded Foreign Secretary Edward Grey that Ministers who objected to men in the field such as Shakespear telling them the truth as they saw it, because it conflicted with their own policies and prejudices, did no service to government or themselves. I sometimes feel that those words should be writ large in all office of state. It was, of course, simply a new aspect of the old struggle between India and the Home government, between the India Office and the Foreign Office.

Thirty years after Gladstone's 'bag and baggage' speech, Britain still insisted on maintaining the status quo in central Arabia and the Gulf, and warned its own representatives not to become entangled in the politics of the area. France and Germany had no such qualms. Thus began the era of clandestine travel, in which Britons travelling in those parts often had the tacit support of one department of state but not of another. An era in which Germany already had the most effective 'Nachrichtdienst' or news-service (a much more apt word than 'intelligence') and was gradually usurping Britain's commercial dominance of the Gulf.

As so often happens, fate took a decisive hand. I need waste no time in telling this audience that in the very early days of the new century, the warrior king Abdul-Aziz retook his capital from its Rashid governor, and thus the re-emergence and transformation of Najd into a strong and ambitious Saudi Arabia began. It was an event the significance of which took a little time to seep into the European mind, but it soon began to concentrated political minds.

Nowhere was the realisation of change in central Arabia better portrayed in its earliest stages than in the brief drama acted out by the gallant Shakespear and his rival on the scene, Lieutenant Gerard Leachman, representing as they did opposite extremes of Britain's imperial presence – one the Indian Political Service, the other a staff officer of the British army on 'special duty'.

Shakespear was of course a creature of the Raj, confirmed through generations of his family. They had been pillars of the Indian empire for generations past, surviving and succeeding through the ups and downs of the Company, the Mutiny and the power conflicts between political and military wings of the viceroys' administrations. Close relatives were high officials in Calcutta and Simla. His father worked for the Bengal forestry service. His mother, a descendant of English - West Indian slave traders, was the dominant parent. And by the time he was ready for school it was one of the up and coming public schools with a reputation for taking on the progeny of empire that

attracted his devoted mother, King William's College in the Isle of Man. 'Shakers' left school with a modest academic record and an all-round sporting presence, especially on the rugby and cricket fields. Sandhurst led straight to India and reunion with the family. He learnt Arabic and Farsi, and was soon in demand as an interpreter and translator. Thus his passage from the Devonshire Regiment to the Bengal Lancers and thence into the Indian political service was determined. Shakespear became the youngest political officer in the service when in 1904 at the age of 25 he was appointed Consul and PO at Bandar Abbas. He was also made first assistant Resident to Cox at Bushire. Five years later he was in Kuwait at the court of Mubarak bin Sabah. From then on he moved freely among those classless stalwarts of the desert, the Badu and their leaders, and among the seafarers of the Gulf. He won the friendship and admiration of both but he kept them at arm's length. He was ever the Englishman abroad. The 'stiff upper lip' was always prominent. Arabs were always amused to see him retire to bathe privately in the special compartment of his tent designed for the purpose, or taking his meals in splendid isolation, usually with a glass of Moselle to hand, eating his lamb with a strange greenish fluid or a red jam-like substance, putting on weight as the years rolled by, while they, the Badawin, the most gregarious of humans, lived and ate in heaps and told endless tales round the evening fire. In the context of this exhibition, I should add that when night and darkness fell on the desert he used the 'bathroom' section of his tent as his photographic dark-room, developing the pictures he had taken od people and places. I suspect that it was his independence, his determination to retain his identity as a British officer, unlike others before and after him who tried to assume Arab dress and habits, that most appealed to Bin Saud. As Shakespear would soon learn, the Saudi leader had a keen eye for the genuine man and distrusted those who temporised with their beliefs or faith.

What of Leachman? Lijman of the Arabs could not have been more different. Lanky,

wiry, ascetic, capable of going for days with little food or water, ruthless, fearless, and cavalier. His physician father put him through the powerhouse of Charterhouse School without laying claim to a single distinction, academic or sporting, though he just made it to Sandhurst and left there in time to serve bravely and with some distinction in the Boer War. Unlike Shakespear, he learnt Arabic not from books and teachers but from the vernacular of the Badawin. By the time their paths crossed in Arabia, the two men already represented separate sides in the Calcutta–Whitehall dispute. None-the-less, they had a common interest: Britain's role in the Arabian peninsula. It was a role dictated by the incursions of France, Germany and Austria-Hungary into what was hitherto regarded as British India's extended back garden – even if it did belong to the empire of the Ottoman Turks. Arab leaders were already starting out on the road to statehood, making up their minds as to which imperial power best represented their interests. 'The Illicit Adventure', is a term I borrowed from that unashamed imperialist Lord Milner to portray the ebb and flow of events at this time. He said that Britain's policy from the outset was to diddle France out of Syria. That certainly became Lloyd George's policy a few years later. I would remind the noble lord however, if he is looking down from his heavenly perch, that Syria belonged neither to France nor Britain, though neither is very good at remembering that Saladin won the battle for Jerusalem.

I must desist from politics, at any rate contemporary politics, lest I am carried away – save to say one thing – that in the aftermath of events in which three of my subjects, Shakespear, Leachman and Gertrude Bell, were intimately involved, Britain in 1914, through the Anglo-Turkish Convention, retained its Kuwait cockpit in the Persian Gulf, while Abdul-Aziz in Riyadh was thrown to the Turkish wolves, recognised by Britain as the Ottoman power's kaimakam, or local governor, a position that Abdul-Aziz vigorously rejected.

Happily there have been refreshing

supplements to my versions of events, which, like all such matters, are subjective in their recording. Most importantly, there was an Arab view penned by the late Amir of the northern Saudi province of Al Jauf, His Highness Abdurrahman al Sudairy, which put my conclusions under an expert, perceptive and kindly magnifying glass. It was one of the Amir's uncles, Abdul Mehsin As-Sudairi, who was Shakespear's generous host in the Sudair townships in 1914. On a personal note, it was as the result of a visit to Jauf at the invitation of the Amir Abdurahman, that I was able to fly over almost the whole of Shakespear's overland route from Riyadh to Al Jauf, to sort out some complex questions of local geography and to sit aloft the splendid toytown Kasr Marid where Shakespear was received by Nuri bin Shalaan and his son Nawaf during the former's tenancy of the town.

And there is a new book by Anne al Bassam that has won much praise in the Gulf region but has yet to make headway north and west, and indeed here in Britain. It is called *Footsteps in the Sand*. It pays handsome acknowledgement to my books – a courtesy that is not, I regret to say, universal – and I am delighted to be able to return the compliment. Mrs Bassam is of course the wife of Bassam Abdullah Saleh Al Bassam, representative of an Arab family that was host to Charles Doughty during his unhappy visit to Nejd, and has been privy to the journeys of just about every European who set foot in Syria, Iraq and the Arabian Peninsula from the mid-19th century to the days of the Cadillac and the 4 by 4. Anne Bessam has woven my tales into a fascinating account of Eastern Arabian history and added grace notes of her own. Using her sequence of events I am able to cut a few corners.

Strangely, Shakespear and Leachman were destined never to meet, though they would come within shouting distance of each other in the desert region between Kuwait and Najd, and would engage in angry personal conflict over Leachman's incursions into the Kuwait territory that Shakespear had been sent to guard as Britain's strong man in the

region.

Leachman and Shakespear both made their first excursions in the Arabian desert in the last days of 1909. Leachman had been on the 'Special Duty' list for two years, most of it spent in India. His Arabian exploit was preceded by a visit to London and MO 2 (a), military intelligence in those days being part of the Military Operations directorate. His task was to reach Hail in disguise if he could and assess the strength and stability of the regime that the Turks and Britain regarded as the dominant power in Najd. He headed from Baghdad to Najaf, disguised in Arab dress, in company with a party of Shammar. They proceeded along the Darb Zobaidah, the pilgrim path that led to Hail and Madina. Shakespear followed in much the same direction. In defiance of Whitehall's injunction that he should not become involved in the affairs of the Amir of Riyadh, he headed out of Kuwait, coming close to the tribal territory that Leachman was making for. Thus he was able to keep in touch with the desert grapevine as his fellow countryman passed close by. Leachman was being followed not only by his compatriot, however, but by the very able Austrian spy Alois Musil, a Jewish academic who was the eyes and ears in Arabia of the developing alliance between the empires of Germany, Austria-Hungary and Turkey. Austria was already instrumental in sending arms supplies to Bin Rashid at Hail. For Shakespear and the Indian government it was a matter that should be addressed before it led to irreversible change in the balance of power in central Arabia. At any rate, three men, representing diverse interests and major powers that would be at war with each other within three years, were at this moment in Februaray 1910, at the epicentre of tribal politics. What was happening here in a desert region that saw some of the early 20th century tussles between tribes loyal to As-Saud and Ar-Rashid would lead to alliances and contracts that would determine the emerging map of the Arabian peninsula.

Leachman and his company of Baghdadi adventurers left Karbala on 26 January 1910. After a week or so on the open road they

were enjoying the spree. They were mounted on ponies, Leachmman's long legs touching the ground for he had no stirrups, causing much amusement. They expected to excite no more interest than would any small group of Arab travellers on the road so generously provided with watering places in the 4th century of the Hegira, by Harun Rashid's Queen.

Imagine then their surprise when they were suddenly confronted by a posse of armed camel riders sent by the Anaiza sheikh Fahad Beq, sworn enemy of the Rashid force he intended to visit, to take them to his camp in protective custody. Imagine, furthermore, the surprise of this English agent when he and his companions found themselves in very short time at a vast Anaiza encampment that stretched as far as the eye could see, occupied by an army that was also on its way to invade Hail, home of the Rashid and the fortress capital of Jabal Shammar.

But that wasn't the end of this volley of surprise. In very short time our group of adventurers had other captors. Leachman was quite unprepared for the sudden appearance of the Shammar under the very able leadership of the latest Ibn Rashid, the Regent Zamil Subhan. The Anaiza encampment was thoroughly ransacked by rampaging horsemen. The Englishman and his Shammari friends escaped the sword-brandishing Shammar and were taken to the new conqueror's tent.

There seems to have been some extensive planning by the Anaiza. Not long before Fahad Beq's force proceeded towards Hail, another Anaiza army, its western arm led by the paramount chief of the Ruwalla faction of the mighty Anaiza, Nuri bin Shaalan of whom I spoke a few moments ago, had captured the strategically important northern town of Jauf from the Rashid. Leachman somehow dispatched a letter by desert messenger to his rival Shakespear in Kuwait, telling him the story thus far. Remember it was their first communication.

Dear Shakespear

I know you by name from Gibbon in the Intelligence at Simla. I am here at camp with Ibn Rashid near Hail. Three days ago I was with a very large mass of the Anaiza on their way to attack Ibn Rashid. In the evening Rashid appeared and utterly defeated the Anaiza who got away with their camels only. Rashid's men looted thousands of tents.

He told Shakespear how he had escaped with his friends and had joined up with the victorious Shammar at Zamil's HQ. The Rashid regent wanted the news of his victory to 'resound widely'. Zamil had spared the Anaiza chief, said Leachman, 'always insisting the enemy chiefs should not be harmed'.

Leachman was much impressed by Zamil Subhan who he said had 'the straight gaze of an honest man'. He also met the boy prince of Hail, Saud bin Abdal Aziz ar-Rashid and found him an 'attractive if ill-tempered youth' of about 12 years, whose only apparent interest was in horses. Until recently he had been in the care of the Sharif of Mecca. The Englishman sought permission to go on to Hail but Zamil refused him but allowed him to join the Shammar army at its camp at Shahiyah where he was granted further interviews with Zamil and the boy prince Saud.

It was two months later, in April, that he was allowed to leave the Shammar camp and make his way back to Baghdad. It was not by any means an ignominious end to an 'intelligence' mission. Indeed, for a young soldier on a covert mission it was a remarkable stroke of fortune that he had been able by sheer chance to speak with the ruler of a large part of central Arabia. It was sufficient to cause Shakespear to make an envious response when the Turks and Shaikh Mubarak questioned Sir Percy Cox about Leachman's presence among the great tribal assembly in Qasim. Shakespear told the Shaikh and his chief that he was not 'enamoured of Leachman's imposture in the desert'. Britain's consul F.E. Crowe was more

discreet. Asked by the Turk governor what Leachman was doing he replied 'he's an English dervish studying botany'.

When the adventure was over, Leachman wrote to John Gordon Lorimer, that most informed of British Political Residents in Baghdad. In that letter, he told Lorimer: 'This movement of the Anaiza was concerted with Bin Saud with the idea of utterly finishing the Rashid power.' It was less than half the story. Zamil Subhan was well disposed to Bin Saud. Indeed, the two men had great respect for each other, and had the former survived assassination at the hands of his own kin, it is not inconceivable that an alliance would have been forged.

While Lijman remained at the camp of Ibn Rashid, Shakespear was dealing with matters closer to home. Shaikh Mubarak and the man he called his 'son', Bin Saud, were also on the warpath. Back in Kuwait in March 1910, with Leachman's adventure still very much in mind, the Political Agent went out to the fortress of Jahra in time to witness a remarkable gathering of tribes. A massive encampment of tents both black and while signalled the presence of large forces of Bin Saud's and Shaikh Mubarak's men, the latter under the leadership of the Shaikh's son Jabir, along with Ajman tribesmen who were making their peace with the Kuwaiti leader after recent raids on his subjects.

Shakespear was convinced that Abdal Aziz, Mubarak, and Bin Hithlain of the Ajman, having waited on the outcome of the battle between the Anaiza and Shammar warriors, were about to launch a fresh attack on the Shammar. As it happened they came face to face with the 4,000 horsemen of the highly disciplined Muntafiq army of Sadun Pasha. The conflict was over almost as soon as it was joined. The Kuwaiti force took flight and lost almost all its arms and animals. The Saudi and Ajman forces fought for a while but the flight of the Kuwaitis left them hopelessly exposed and they too gave up the struggle and hurried back to Kuwait, often five or six to a camel, for Sadun had decreed that his men should take as many animals and arms as they could transport, but that the men themselves should be

spared.

There wasn't much that Shakespear could do about it. He had kept a watching brief at the rear of the Kuwaiti force, but he was told sternly when Whitehall heard about the fiasco 'You will see that the Government of India direct that a warning be conveyed to Shaikh Mubarak, in terms of a previous warning, not to enter into any operations calculated to involve him in difficulties in Najd or with the Turks.' But it was, as they say, game set and match to Leachman, who on the instruction of Zamil Subhan had joined up with the Muntafiq and was by now on terms of close friendship with Sadun Pasha and the Rashid leadership of Hail, while Shakespear was left holding the prickly pear of Mubarak and Kuwait. When he went out to Jahra to deliver HM Government's latest warning to Mubarak, the Shaikh was already gathering another raiding force, hoping to repay the Muntafiq. He attributed his men's defeat not to his son's leadership but to a dust storm. The old Shaikh of Kuwait was described by Lovat Fraser, the well-informed editor of *The Times of India*, as the Richelieu of Arabia. Not a bad comparison. The planned retribution, launched on 1st April 1910, was no more effective than the last. But it was to be Sadun's final victory. Shortly after, the great leader of the Muntafiq confederation of Southern Iraq's Shi'a tribes was invited aboard a gunboat by Sayyid Talib, the son of the Naqib of Basra. There he was handed over to the Turks and sent to imprisonment at Haleb. He was found dead early in 1911, supposedly from poisoning.

In outlining the events of that brief period of 1910, the months from February to April, I have tried to portray as a vividly as I am able the circumstances in which two of the most spirited and courageous figures of the British administration came into close proximity in the early years of the last century, in tribal forays that were beginning to excite the interest of the imperial powers of Europe, without ever meeting. Both were destined to die before wartime promises made by Britain and France to each other, to the Zionists and to Arab leaders came to haunt them. Before the ultimate ascendancy of Bin Saud, which Shakespear alone among Britain's representatives predicted, determined a large part of the map of the Middle East.

Leachman, I need hardly say, ended the war as the most admired of British soldiers in what was then Mesopotamia. One of the few men who observed his wartime feats in the depths of the tribal territory of the Shammar and Anaiza and Muntafiq, was the air ace Geoffrey de Havilland, then a Major in the Royal Flying Corps. He flew routinely over the deserts where Leachman was engaged with Fahad Beq's Anaiza, alongside the tribe's own sheikhs, in the war against the Turks. He wrote: 'The story of this Englishman may never be written, yet in the history of the world there is probably no romance that can equal it.' A tall claim you may say, but one that de Havilland stood by. Fahad Beq Hadhhal, the man who had arrested him to protect him from the Shammar on the hajj road to Hail, became Britain's wartime ally, and he said of Leachman, 'He was just one of us, like one of our shaikhs'. It must all seem very convoluted to some of you. How alliances and loyalties can change!

Leachman became the first military governor of Kurdistan after the war, but he was deemed by the Civil Commissioner too tough and rough even for the Kurds. In 1920, he was the victim of an assassin's bullet in Falluja, a name that has acquired a new resonance in recent times.

Shakespear, of course, was vindicated by Turkey's decision to join the Great War on Germany's side. Just before that war broke out he made his famous trans-Arabian journey, in the course of which his guide Saleh al Mutawah disappeared on the road to Zarud in the borderland of Jabal Shammar and Qasim, later to return with the news that Zamil Subhan, the only man who could have brought peace between the houses of al Saud and al Rashid, had been murdered by slaves of the young prince Saud ibn Rashid.

Early in 1915. Shakespear was sent back to Najd by Whitehall to encourage Bin Saud's anti-Turk campaign – a campaign that he had so recently been told to discourage. And as we know he was killed within weeks of Britain's expeditionary force landing at Basra, fighting alongside Bin Saud in yet another battle with the Shammar army. It was a tragic end for a man who had so much to offer the Anglo-Saudi cause. It is I think a perfect epitaph that after his death it was discovered that he had made arrangements with the Government of India for a light aircraft to be made available to him, so that he could make the journey from the Gulf to Riyadh in an hour or two. He had motored from Bushire to England in 1910 in a single-cylinder car. Pioneer motorist and aviator, skilled yachtsman, he was the schoolboy's image of the English hero in foreign fields. But it took a long time for the grown up world of politics and diplomacy to recognise his remarkable qualities. What a magnificent first British ambassador to the court of Bin Saud he would have made, and with what honour he would have been received in Riyadh. Inshallah.

I have left almost to the last reference to one of the most important contributions made to our understanding of central Arabia by these disparate Englishmen. Their photography, much of it as you see for yourselves today, of historic importance. In my books I record in detail the movements of Shakespear, Leachman and the Dane Raunkiaer in 1911, when all of them, naming the Royal Geographical Societies of England and Denmark as their patrons, made applications to visit Riyadh. Unfortunately, we do not have the Dane's pictorial record. The two Englishmen, however, always travelled with camera at the ready. Shakespear had to be content with a first meeting with the Amir Abdal Aziz in Kuwait, at Shaikh Mubaraks palace, and a few weeks later at Thaj in Al Hasa. There he was able to take some fine pictures of the Saudi leader and his brothers and sons, several of them destined to become sovereign rulers of the Kingdom. As far as I know, they and the Kuwait pictures were the first ever taken of the Saudi royal family. At any rate, they were certainly the best, taken on that elaborate and heavy plate camera that went everywhere with him, along with the developing facilities that turned his tent into something between a pharmacy and a source of entertainment for the Badu. Of course a dark room was essential. It was no small achievement to develop film in the desert, indeed anywhere else, in those days. His glass negatives in the RGS are as sharp and clear today as they were on the day of their development a century ago. The Shakespears, as it happens, were closely related to the Fox Talbots. His brother Henry carried the second name Talbot.

Leachman who eventually arrived in Riyadh on Christmas Eve 1912, nine months after Raunkiaer, took what must have been the earliest photos of the capital. And he went on to join the Amir at camp and take more pictures. If the results were not markedly professional or dramatic, they were very good indeed considering the time and circumstances in which they were taken.

It would take Shakespear another year to obtain Whitehall's permission to follow in Leachman's footsteps. Mortified by the news of his fellow countryman's successful visit, he responded with a not exactly fulsome tribute: 'I'm awfully pleased that Ibn Saud did him so well, though I rather envy those other travellers going to Riyadh when I'm the only one who really knows the king'. Between them the two men made what was for their time a unique record of life in the desert, the townships of Qasim and Aridh and Jabal Shammar. But as we see, when he eventually reached Riyadh he made a very detailed record of life in what was then the capital township of Najd. But of course, a heavy tripod camera requiring a separate glass plate for each exposure was not the ideal way of taking snap photos. To see Shakespear's photography at its best, it is necessary to look at his magnificent time coverage of the 1911 Delhi Durbar marking the coronation of Edward VII, some of which is to be found in my biography.

I have hardly mentioned my two Ladies of the Arab lands. We always call Anne Blunt 'Lady Anne' since she was a 'Lady' by birth. She was the pioneer woman of desert exploration, the first of her sex to reach central Arabia, yet she was dominated by an irascible, arrogant, vain husband.

In contrast, Gertrude Bell, Anne's successor at Hail and along the Euphrates, was a woman who dominated the male world she inhabited by the force of her intellect. But she would most certainly have preferred marriage and family life had her powerful opinions not stood in the way of any such contract. They succeeded each other too in wearing that rather strange Turco-Arabic courtesy label 'Al Khatun', a title that denoted a lady of esteem in their midst. If they were so different as women, they were remarkably alike in strength of mind and in their stoicism as travellers.

Anne was of course the granddaughter of Lord Byron and that tedious wife of his, the 'Princess of Parallelograms'. She was daughter of Ada, Countess of Lovelace, she of the poet's 'house and heart', whose contribution to the development of computer science is recognised to this day in the code name of the Pentagon's secret language, Ada. More to the point of this talk, she was the first European of her sex to make a recorded journey into Central Arabia. Her passion, of course, was the Arab horse, and she devoted much of her life to its salvation at her famous Crabbet stud in Sussex. Between times she translated into English some of the finest pre-Islamic verse, including the celebrated tale of Abu Zaid al-Hilali and the Stealing of the Mare, wrote two books recording the journeys she and her husband made to Najd and the Euphrates Valley which remain in print to this day, and – as we see today - displayed very real ability as a watercolourist. For Anne's determined grandmother, in whose care she was raised, only the best tutors were good enough. Her drawing master was Ruskin no less. Joachim taught her the violin, Hallé gave her piano lessons. Certainly the influence of Ruskin, and of his idol Turner, is evident in some of the work you see here today, photographs of those delightful watercolour sketches made in he notebooks as she went in search of the tribes and the pedigree horses of Arabia. Her skill with pencil and brush is obvious, but

there the comparison ends. In art as in life, the charming, attractive lady with the melodious voice said to come from her grandfather and the aristocratic demeanour, lacked imagination above all else. Her drawing had charm but not life force. She won for herself a reputation for bravery and perseverance in the face of hazard and hardship that persists to this day in many parts of the Arab world. Her Arabic was good enough to keep up a correspondence with Arab ulema across thirty years or more.

It was, I thought, a life that deserved biographical recognition, even if it did lack some of the scandalous attributes that have become distinct biographical merits in some of the aristocratic ladies on her husband's visiting list. But it took me more than twenty years to find a publisher who shared my view. If only she had emulated her husband's nocturnal history; what a publishing appeal that would have had.

It is apparent from what has gone before that the years 1910 to 1912 were a busy period in the complex interrelationship between the European powers and the Ottoman territories. Impending war was in the air. It was on 18 March 1911 that T.E. Lawrence, newly arrived as an apprentice archaeologist at the site of Jerabalus, or Carchemish, wrote to his bother to say 'We are expecting a Miss G. Bell'. The world knew little of either of them at that time, though Gertrude had published two well-received books and was the better known. It was a time of intense archaeology and widespread espionage. The two came together almost inevitably. At such places as Carchemish, Nineveh, Ashur, Babylon, learned spies proliferated, soon to become staff officers in their respective armies. Miss G. Bell was one of them.

Gertrude's contribution to the political make up of the modern Middle East may have its detractors. But of her contribution to the western world's understanding of civilisations of the Middle East there can be no question. You will see from the work on display here that her contribution to the pictorial record of Najd and other Arab lands before the First World War was immense.

More than anyone, she caught the Badawin, those most serious and solemn of humans, off guard. She worked with faster film and more responsive cameras of the Rolleiflex and Leica variety. Of course, she could afford the best cameras that money could buy. For almost the whole of her life she travelled as the favoured daughter of one of the wealthiest families in England, owners of steel, aluminium, chemical and coal enterprises. Only in the year of her death, 1926, were there signs that the solid fortune that underpinned her life of travel and adventure was on the wane. Had she lived for just another year she would have seen the sale of her beloved home, Rounton Grange in North Yorkshire, with its Morris and Burne-Jones decoration and the garden that she had so fondly created.

As Rebecca West wrote of her: 'she was the incarnation of the emancipated heiress, using the gold given her by the industrial revolution to buy not privilege but the opportunity for noble performance'. Rebecca West saw in her the realisation of Charlotte Brontë's 'Shirley'.

She was indeed, as both Arab and British admirers pointed out, a woman of great valour, and remarkable intellect. Her visit to Hail certainly demanded that combination of features, and more. There is little doubt in my mind that her visit to the Rashid capital a few months before the outbreak of world war had obvious undertones of espionage. Perhaps she was favoured by the absence of the Rashid princes on one of their not infrequent bouts of regicide. At any rate she escaped from 'house' imprisonment to reach Baghdad safely. A year later, as titular head of the Arab Bureau in Basra – as L.S. Amery never tired of telling us, the first woman officer of Britain's military intelligence service – she set in motion that train of events that would lead to Britain's adoption of the Sharifian family of Husain bin Ali as the princes of all the conquered Arab lands, though France prevented their realisation in Greater Syria. And of course, the stewardship of Iraq and Transjordan, was counterbalanced by the victorious progress of Bin Saud in central Arabia. To that most masculine and powerful of Arabian leaders, Gertrude was, to put it mildly, an enigma.

There is something very poignant in the contemporary context in speaking today of her unique contribution to Al-'Iraq as she punctiliously called it; to the preservation of Iraq's heritage, indeed the world's heritage, through the libraries and museums she created and the artefacts she safeguarded. She had an almost uncanny sense of archaeology and ancient history. She was admired as much by the learned men of the Deutsche Orient Gesellshaft, as by their British counterparts who dug under her auspices. By the time Leonard Woolley arrived Ur in 1921 she was able to stand on fairly level ground with him. At that time she had only her first Baghdad Museum with its single exhibition room to fill. By the time Woolley's expedition was in its fourth year she had a new and luxurious space to fill. The government King Faisal I, advised by Gertrude, was only too anxious to ensure that it had the lion's share of the finds of Ur.

By the 1920s the scene was set for Gertrude's annual visits to Woolley's lair at Ur and to that of Langdon of Oxford who was working at Kish at the same time. And the expedition was given literary immortality by the presence of no less popular a writer than Agatha Christie who had gone there to recover from her famous disappearance, only to meet, and later to marry, Woolley's assistant Max Mallowan. Perhaps the human side of these excavations was best exemplified by Mallowan's description of the bizarre relationship with the widowed lady Woolley brought to the site in 1924, Katherine Keeling, a woman so domineering and determined to have her own way that almost all the men present were fearful of crossing her or of entering into the smallest argument with her. Ur was a joint venture between the British and Philadelphia museums and, needless to say, the directors of both institutions were very concerned about the lady's omnipresence and her possible effect on the morale of the archaeological teams there. When Woolley eventually took her with him to England and married her he spent his wedding night sleeping in an

armchair while she locked herself in the bathroom. It is said that the marriage was never consummated. Mallowan described hilariously the night scene back in Ur where the two occupied separate bedrooms, Woolley with a length of string attached to his little finger while he slept, the string leading along the corridor and into her bed, so that she could pull on it to awaken him when one of her nightly attacks of migraine came on. Poor Woolley would always go to her aid, even though he had often worked a 14–hour day in dust and heat and desperately needed sleep.

We also owe to Max the story of Gertrude's annual visit in 1924 to supervise the distribution of the season's find's. She had insisted on having for her Baghdad museum a particularly precious piece. She was accompanied by Lionel Smith, Dean of Magdalen, and tutor to Edward VIII (though I don't suppose he boasted of that) Woolley argued ferociously that the piece should go either to the BM or to Philadelphia, but Gertrude was insistent and the last word was hers. The dignified Smith put in a mild word or two on Woolley's behalf. As they departed for Ur junction to catch their train to Baghdad, Max and Agatha heard Gertrude muttering between clenched teeth, 'You traitor! You traitor!'.

Then there were the colourful descriptions of daily life at that remarkable Anglo-American archaeological site, as that formidable foreman Hamoudi commanded his workforce of Marsh Arabs. Hamoudi, always high above his workforce, flapping his arms like an Eagle in the cool of the evening, 'like a proud eagle', as Max Mallowan put it, sending shadows scudding across the sandy plain, 'ready to swoop on his prey', cajoling, laughing, sympathising, ridiculing. 'To command a man must be loved and feared' he always insisted. And there was a description by another visitor, a master at Clifton School, of Hamoudi leading the entertainment as his men tired at the end of a long day. He would burst into song and take on the role of a marsh boatman as he used his spade as a punt pole, and the evening air resounded to the chants of the

men as they swayed in rhythmic imitation of a night journey in their long swift skiffs. As he said, he and Woolley had broken much bread together.

Again, I liked Agatha's autobiographical words: 'I fell in love with Ur, with its beauty in the evenings, the ziggurat standing up, faintly shadowed, and that wide area of sand with its lovely pale colours of apricot, rose, blue and mauve changing every minute…the lure of the past came up to grab me…I was filed with a longing to be an archaeologist…How unfortunate it was, I thought, that I had always led such a frivolous life…'.

Such are the sidelights of our story. It is appropriate that I should end this talk with mention of my subjects' observations on the land of our hosts, the Kingdom of Saudi Arabia as it would become after their deaths.

It is I think true to say that if Shakespear and Leachman had one thing in common – and it was about the only thing they had in common – it was an unqualified admiration for the founder of the Kingdom. Among my men and women, Shakespear was the first to venture a portrait of the great man, following Bin Saud's visit to Kuwait in February 1910. It was a brief description contained in his official report to the India Office. 'Abdul Aziz, now in his 31st year', he wrote, 'is fair, handsome and considerably above average Arab height… He has a frank open face and, after initial reserve, is of genial and courteous manner'. If nothing else, a succinct and accurate miniature portrait.

Leachman was next in line. To Shakespear's chagrin he travelled from Damascus to Riyadh in 1913 in what must have been record time in its day, a little over five weeks, with one of two brothers, Saleh Mutawah as his guide. The al-Mutawah seem from my researches to have been close to both the Saud and Rashid families. It was the same Saleh for whom Shakespear waited in vain at Zarud when Zamil Subhan was in mortal danger in 1914. Leachman arrived with Saleh Mutawah at what he described as 'the high gateway' of Riyadh, presumably the entrance to the Saudi palace with its iron-studded wooden doors, on 25 December, 1913.

'We passed through a number of quiet by-streets and then suddenly emerged into a broad square with a bazaar, in which business was at its height at this noontide hour of the day,' Leachman reported. 'As we passed through, many curious eyes were fixed on us, and then we came to a large open space flanked on the right by a lofty castle, which proved to be the palace of Abdal Aziz ibn Saud, Amir of Najd'.

He was greeted warmly by the Amir and wrote afterwards:

'He is a man of about forty, six feet high and broad in proportion, with a strong though kindly face and the simplest of manners. He shook me by the hand and put me at my ease at once by the friendliness of his greeting.'

Leachman spoke of the Amir's courtesy and said that stories of Wahhabist fanaticism were ill founded. He went on to recite Bin Saud's account of the storming of Riyadh in 1902. It is a story that is of course enshrined in the annals of central Arabia and needs no repetition here. Shakespear had heard the same story at camp at Thaj in 1912.

When Shakespear reached Riyadh on 11 May 1914, he camped in the date garden outside the town. He never accepted the shelter of his hosts. In his report to the Viceroy after that visit he described his entry into Riyadh:

'…went by moonlight along the Shaib until we crossed a bit of rising ground and the whole east wall of the town with its bastions was in front. Taken through east gate along a wide road, past a lot of ruins and some big houses built on a palatial scale…Greeted warmly. Tea, coffee and sweets until evening prayer.'

Then of his host:

'Abdul-Aziz is a broad-minded and straight man…His reputation is that of a noble and generous man…'

He spoke of the enmity Abdul-Aziz felt

for the Turks who then occupied al Hasa, and of the Arab leader's desire for friendship with Britain. Contrary to most received opinion, Shakespear thought that Palgrave's plan of Riyadh was 'exceedingly good'. And it is worth noting that he differed radically from Philby with regard to Palgrave's description of Ayun, the Arabian 'Stonehenge', again finding it accurate, if sparce.

Almost the entire male family of Bin Saud joined the Englishman on the second day of his visit in the palm grove of Shamsiyah, the garden mad by Mahbub, prime minister of Bin Saud's grandfather Faisal bin Turki. The Englishman was able to photograph the procession of sons, several of whom would inherit the throne of the kingdom – Fahd and Muhammad, Turki, Saud, and Faisal. And he was to speak in report after report to his government of the Saudi leader's 'sincerity and utter reliability', of his single-minded devotion to his people and his religion', and to the securing of their independence from Turkish imperial rule. But it was not until war was declared that Whitehall took his offer of alliance seriously if a little churlishly.

Neither of our Englishmen shone as writers outside the strict realm of official reporting. It was left to Gertrude to fill in the interim with her customary zest.

Gertrude, as we know, became, in her own words, a Sharifian through and through, but that made little impact on the Saudi leader. Abdul-Aziz for his part was never able to take very seriously the belief of this determined English lady that she could single handedly determine the fate of the emerging Arab nations. According to Philby, he often entertained his tribesmen with imitations of a shrill feminine voice calling 'Abdul-Aziz, look at this'or at that or the other. But hers was the most generous and most vivid of all the pen portraits to this very day. In fact she wrote two descriptions, the first before she met him at the famous Kuwait durbar, and based on information supplied by the American missionary doctor, Paul Harrison. 'He possesses great personal charm, with a ready and attractive smile. He is a great

kingly-looking man like an Assyrian picture…' And so on, with references to his many wives and children, and some very misleading references to his dealings with other Arab chiefs.

It was the meeting at the subsequent Basra durbar of 1916 that caused Gertrude to write for the Arab Bulletin, the fortnightly journal of the Bureau in Cairo, her famous portrait:

'Ibn Saud is now barely forty, though he looks some years older. He is a man of splendid physique, standing well over six feet, and carrying himself with the air of one accustomed to command. Though he is more massively built than the typical nomad sheikh, he has the characteristics of the well-bred Arab, the strongly-marked aquiline profile, full-flesh nostrils, prominent lips, a long narrow chin accentuated by a pointed beard. His hands are fine, with slender fingers…and in spite of his great height and breadth of shoulder he conveys the impression common enough in the desert of an indefinable lassitude, the secular weariness of an ancient and self-contained people, which has made heavy drafts on its vital forces and borrowed little from beyond its own forbidding frontiers ...'

She wrote of Ibn Saud's deliberate movements, his 'sweet smile and the contemplative glance of heavy lidded eyes'. By then, the eyes had succumbed to the desert glare. Dr Stanley Mylrae, the senior medical man with the American mission, was there too. He had attended Bin Saud once, three years before, and he added:

'Among all the richly dressed Arabs in the room, he was easily the most conspicuous figure. His magnificent bearing still commanded attention. The three years had only increased the attractiveness of his personality, and when presently Sir Percy Cox presented him with the KCIE and the beautiful ornament glittered on his handsome brown cloak, he would have made an unusual subject for an artist.'

As he watched the proceedings, Mylrae was reminded of Mark Twain's description of King Arthur, 'Armour is proud burden, and a man standeth straight in it.' Others have been inclined to describe Bin Saud as the Richard Lionheart of the Arab world, but with the greatest respect I doubt whether our Arab friends are too keen on the analogy.

If there was no artist to hand, he made an imposing subject for the photographer.

Even so, it was Shakespear's camera that had caught the desert king most aptly, especially at Thaj in the youthful vigour of his leadership, just as Gertrude's words would capture the English imagination and finally convince the Liberal government of the day that it would ignore him at its cost. She wrote of his strength and unequalled skill in the saddle, of his physical endurance, 'rare even in hard-bitten Arabia'; and finally, 'such men as he are the exception in any community, but they are thrown up persistently by the Arab race'. A thought for our politicians of today perhaps.

Crossings of the Empty Quarter

These were the journeys made with Bedu companions by Thesiger (1946-47), Philby (1931-32) and Thomas (1930-31)

Leslie McLoughlin

The man who became world famous for making the first crossing was Bertram Thomas who made the journey from Salala to Doha between December 1930 and February 1931. Having begun life as a Post Office official 1908 -1914 he came to know the Arab world, through his army service in Iraq from 1916 onwards. He became a member of the Civil Administration in Iraq, then he moved to Transjordan where he was an assistant to Philby who had become the Chief British Representative in the newly formed Emirate. He was then seconded to Muscat where he was Finance Minister. While serving in Muscat he made frequent journeys on camel-back with Bedu companions and about 1927 conceived the idea of making a journey with the Bedu from Salala northwards, through territory controlled by Bin Saud, to emerge from the Empty Quarter at Doha. By 1930 he had completed his plans but told no one of them except the future Sultan of Oman Sa'eed bin Taimur.

In late December 1930 he struck out into the Sands with his companions knowing that his life was at risk as a Christian and as an 'illegal immigrant': i.e. he had no authorization from Ibn Saud to cross his territory. The route he took was carefully chosen to follow the line of the known wells. Thomas also made elaborate calculations of food and water supplies to be carried, so that the journey was, in effect, not a dangerous one from the point of view of being able to keep body and soul together. The great danger was of discovery by the tribes, especially by what Thomas loosely called the Ikhwan. In the final stages of the journey when he was most at risk of discovery his group was helped by the fact that they were travelling during Ramadan: the Ikhwan were already away from their normal territory, which lay in their path.

Thomas reached Doha with his companions in early February 1931 and his achievement immediately received worldwide acclaim. He published his work on the journey *Arabia Felix* in 1932 and although he was not able to retire happily on the proceeds, as he had hoped, he was able to give up his work in Muscat.

Thomas was again employed in government work during the Second World War when he worked as a British Information Officer in Bahrain and he finished life as the founder and first Director of the Middle East Centre for Arab Studies, which he opened in Jerusalem in 1944, later moving it to Shemlan, Lebanon in 1948.

Philby (Harry St John Philby who later converted to Islam and took the name Abdullah) was born in 1888 in India. He was sent to Riyadh in 1917 to persuade Ibn Saud to take on a more active military role attacking Hail. As soon as Philby came to know the area on the fringes of the Empty Quarter in 1918 he conceived the idea of being the first non-Arab to cross the Sands. He was therefore bitterly disappointed when he learned in 1931 that Thomas had beaten him to it.

Ibn Saud, however, gave him permission in late 1931 to make an exploratory journey from the South to the North and instructed the Governor of the Eastern Province, Abdullah bin Jiluwi to give him every support. This was naturally to include Bedu companions who would guarantee his safety. By early January all was ready and the group set out with a train of no less than 32 camels. The route taken was a meandering one as Philby was insistent on indulging his interest in the flora and fauna, in geology, archaeology, mineralogy, surveying by compass traverse and astronomic observation. The Bedu did not take kindly to the delays imposed, especially as they were travelling during Ramadan.

A notable feature of Philby's journey was that he was constantly at odds with his companions whereas Thomas was the soul of good cheer and clearly had the best of relations with his companions. (Indeed Thesiger met Thomas and the Bedu companions in the 1940s and was struck by how warmly they remembered him.) So bad did the relations with the Bedu become that Philby learned later that they planned at one stage to kill him.

The journey reached its southernmost point at the wells of Shanna where it became clear that the Bedu would not go on. As the planned route lay south through the territory of tribes who were not represented in his group, Philby therefore had to adopt a route east–west and struck out across the Sands in exceptional heat for the month of February. So severe were the conditions that at one point even the camel tried to take shelter in the tents. Eventually Philby was forced to turn back to the east-west starting point. Naifa, a place where the sulphurous water gave all the group severe stomach problems.

During March 1932 the group struggled across totally unexplored country keeping to a route plotted by Philby and doing a great part of their travelling in the early morning, well before dawn. Eventually, 68 days after leaving Hofuf, they reached Sulaiyil after an especially difficult crossing of the Abu Bahr sands.

Philby then completed a leisurely return to Mecca, arriving by truck, not on camel-back, and said his prayers at the Kaaba before arriving home at 9 p.m. on 5 April 1932.

During 1933 he completed the preparation of his book The Empty Quarter with the help of his son, Kim (the future Soviet spy) and thereafter was rightly celebrated as an intrepid and resourceful traveller and explorer. He was later to make many journeys on camel back at the request of Ibn Saud as the first stage in mapping and documenting the enormous unknown territories of what had become the Kingdom of Saudi Arabia.

Sir Wilfred Thesiger came to the Arab world in a quite different way although he shared with Philby and Thomas a background of service with the British armed forces in wartime. Having been born in Addis Abba into a family with strong connections, in Ethiopia and India principally, he developed from an early age a love of exploratory travel, especially in arduous circumstances. He travelled widely in the desert and by the time of the Second World War was ideally equipped to be part of the Long Range Desert Group patrols, which struck at Axis forces in North Africa. He then spent time on active service on secret missions in Syria where he came to know the great nomadic tribes of Badiat Ash-Shaam.

He was offered the chance to explore the Empty Quarter quite by chance in 1945 when he met a UN official engaged in research related to plotting the incidence of Locust breeding grounds. This would require lengthy journeys in the unexplored regions of the Empty Quarter. Thesiger jumped at the opportunity and began a series of journeys in the Hejaz and Asir to familiarise himself before making plans to travel with Bedu companions from the area of Salala northwards.

His first great journey was made in the eastern part of the Arabian Peninsula starting through the Sands of Ghanin in late 1946. With his companions from the Beit Kathir and the Rashid he made the successful crossing of the extraordinarily difficult region of the Urooq Al – Shaiba returning by a circular route via Oman to Salala.

The second crossing was made in the west via Sulaiyil, Layla and Liwa, reaching Abu Dhabi and Buraimi where he became the guest of Shaikh Zayed bin Sultan Al Nahayan for a month, which they spent happily hunting. At Sulaiyil Thesiger was arrested on Ibn Saud's orders and was released only on the intervention of Philby who then set out to meet Thesiger at Layla. This incident showed the great concern which Ibn Saud had to preserve security in his domains.

As the greater part of the Empty Quarter lies in the Kingdom of Saudi Arabia the lecturer devoted some time to discussion of the way in which each of the explorers was affected by the position of King Abdul-Aziz as the founder of the Kingdom. He pointed out that Thomas, as early as 1931, was fully aware, as an official of a neighbouring Arab country, that Ibn Saud had imposed his will on the tribes and had practically eliminated the anarchy produced by uncontrolled raiding. Philby had of course benefited from being given the full backing and protection of Ibn Saud on his journeys. Thesiger, however, had been arrested as an illegal immigrant on the orders of Ibn Saud. The King had, however, shown considerable magnanimity in ordering his release, after the intervention of Philby.

The Travellers

Note on the material presented:

Gathered here are records, from diverse sources, of British travellers to the Arabian peninsula. Doughty and Palgrave, who travelled before the invention of the camera, and who are today remembered for their vivid written accounts of what they experienced, are represented here by excerpts of their writings. Lady Anne Blunt, who recorded her experiences in a series of widely acclaimed watercolour miniatures to accompany her diary, is represented by a selection of her paintings. For the rest, photographic prints have been the medium chosen here, even where travellers have also left fine written accounts, a choice driven by the author's desire to deliver a presentation of Arabia that is visually led.

No single volume can realistically aspire to encompass, comprehensively, so large a subject as the title of this book suggests; what is contained between these pages is a careful selection, designed to be engaging and informative for a wide audience.

William Gifford Palgrave

1826-1888

Above:
William Gifford Palgrave by Julia Margaret Cameron, 1868.

Opposite:
William Gifford Palgrave's Arabian journey, 1862-63.

The life of W.G. Palgrave, soldier, Jesuit, secret agent and diplomat, still arouses controversy more than one hundred years after his death. Following service in the Bombay Native Infantry he became a Catholic and joined the Jesuit order. Having learned Arabic in Lebanon, he set off for Arabia disguised as a Syrian travelling doctor. In 1862 he reached Nejd, where he commented that: "A Christian and an Englishman may well traverse Arabia, and even Nejd, without being ever obliged to compromise either his religion or his honour: but for this, perfect acquaintance with Eastern customs and with at least one Eastern language, together with much circumspection and guardedness in word and deed, are undeniably required."

On entering Hail, Palgrave was kindly received by the Emir, Talal ibn Rashid, who walked hand-in-hand through the town with him. He travelled on to Riyadh, where he was received by members of the Al Saud and the Imam's court, including the Imam's elder son, Emir Abdullah, whom Palgrave described as looking like Henry VIII, and having many of the same characteristics. Leaving Riyadh, he travelled to Hofuf and thence to Bahrain, Qatar and Oman.

In 1865 Palgrave published his *Narrative of a Year's Journey through Central and Eastern Arabia*, which *The Times* described as: "One of the most interesting and romantic books of travel that have ever delighted the public." T.E. Lawrence declared him a brilliant writer and explorer, but H. St J. B. Philby, who covered the same ground as Palgrave, cast doubt on his account, much of which, he said, did not stand up to close scrutiny. We shall never know how much of Palgrave's narrative is true and how much is simply embroidery: as he himself wrote at the end of his book, "much, how much is left untold."

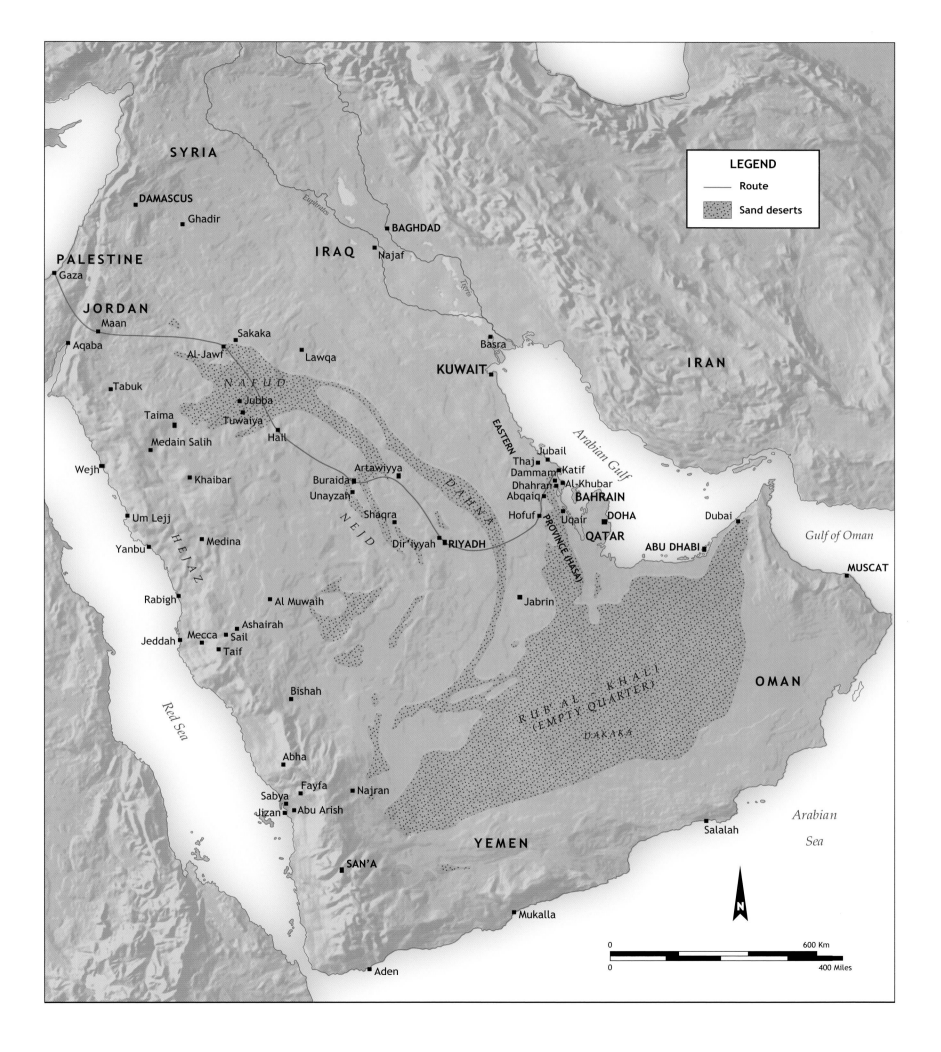

SYRIA

DAMASCUS
Ghadir

BAGHDAD
IRAQ
Najaf

PALESTINE
Gaza

JORDAN
Maan
Aqaba

Sakaka
Al-Jawf
Lawqa

Basra
KUWAIT

Tabuk

N A F U D

Jubba
Tuwaiya
Taima
Hail
Medain Salih

Wejh
Khaibar

D A H N A

Artawiyya
Buraida
Unayzah
Shaqra

Thaj
Dammam
Dhahran
Abqaiq
Hofuf

Jubail
Katif
Al-Khubar
BAHRAIN
DOHA
Uqair
QATAR

Arabian Gulf

Dubai

Um Lejj

Medina
Yanbu

H E J A Z

N E J D

Dir'iyyah RIYADH

EASTERN
PROVINCE (HASA)

ABU DHABI

Gulf of Oman

MUSCAT

Rabigh

Al Muwaih

Jabrin

OMAN

Ashairah
Mecca Sail
Jeddah Taif

Bishah

R U B   A L   K H A L I
(EMPTY QUARTER)
DAKAKA

Red Sea

Abha

Fayfa
Sabya Najran
Jizan Abu Arish

Salalah

Arabian
Sea

YEMEN

SAN'A

Mukalla

Aden

LEGEND
—— Route
Sand deserts

0   600 Km
0   400 Miles

N

3

Extracts from W. G. Palgrave's *Narrative of a Year's Journey through Central and Eastern Arabia*

Palgrave summoned his considerable powers of description to evoke the journey across the desolate Nafud desert in the unforgiving heat of midsummer:

We were now traversing an immense ocean of loose reddish sand, unlimited to the eye, and heaped up in enormous ridges running parallel to each other from north to south, undulation after undulation, each swell two or three hundred feet in average height, with slant sides and rounded crests furrowed in every direction by the capricious gales of the desert. In the depths between, the traveller finds himself as it were imprisoned in a suffocating sand-pit, hemmed in by burning walls on every side; while at other times, while labouring up the slope he over looks what seems a vast sea of fire, swelling under a heavy monsoon wind, and ruffled by a cross-blast into little red-hot waves. Neither shelter nor rest for eye or limb amid torrents of light and heat poured from above on an answering glare.

On the night journey as they first cross into the sands of the Nefud:

All night, a weary night, we waded up and down through waves of sand, in which the camels often sank up to their knees, and their riders were obliged to alight and help them on. There was no symptom of a track, no landmark to direct our way; the stars alone now were our compass and guide; but Aboo-'Eysa had passed this Nefood more than once, and knew the line of march by heart. When the first pale streak of dawn appeared on our right shoulder, we were near the summit of a sandy mountain, and the air blew keener than I had yet felt in Arabia. We halted and gathered together heaps of Ghada and other desert shrubs to light blazing fires, by which some sat, some lay and slept, myself for one, till the rising sunbeams tipped the yellow crests around, and we resumed our way.

Here, he describes the Emir Talal ibn Rashid, whom he considered the ideal Arab ruler:

The young sovereign possessed in fact, all that Arab ideas require to ensure good government and lasting popularity. Affable towards the common people, reserved and haughty with the aristocracy, courageous and skilful in war, a lover of commerce and building in time of peace, liberal even to profusion, yet always careful to maintain and augment the state revenue, neither over-strict nor yet scandalously lax in religion, secret in his designs, but never known to break a promise once given, or violate a plighted faith; severe in administration, yet averse to bloodshed, he offered the very type of what an Arab prince should be.

On reaching Riyadh, "the capital of Najd and half Arabia, its very heart of hearts", Palgrave stood at the great doorway of the royal palace:

Deep sunk between the bastions, with massive folding-doors iron-bound, though thrown open at this hour of the day, and giving entrance into a dark passage, one might easily have taken it for the vestibule of a prison; while the number of guards, some black, some white, but all sword-girt, who almost choked the way, did not seem very inviting to those without, especially to foreigners. Long earth-seats lined the adjoining walls, and afforded a convenient waiting-place for visitors; and here we took up our rest at a little distance from the palace gate.

On impressions of the townspeople of Riyadh:

Amid the rabble are many other elements, exotic to Ri'ad, though never wholly absent from it. Camel drivers from Zulphah, who in their frequent intercourse with Zobeyr and Basrah have alloyed Wahhabee gravity and Nejdean decency with the devil-may-care way of those ambiguous lands half Shiya'ee, half infidel; som ill-conditioned youth, who having run away with his father or the Metow'waa' at Ri'ad, has awhile sought liberty and fortune among the sailors of Koweyt or Taroot, and returned with morals and manners worthy of Wapping or Portsmouth; some thin Yemanee pedlar, come up by Wadi Nejran and Dowasir to slip quietly in and out through the streets of the capital and laugh at all he sees; perhaps some Belooch or Candahar darweesh, like those who accompanied us a month ago to Bereydah, and who here awaits companions with whom to cross the eastern arm of the desert on his way to the Persian Gulf; mixed with these the beggars of Dowasir, more fanatic, more viciously ill-tempered, and more narrow in heart and head than the men of 'Aared themselves, with the addition of laziness, meanness, and avarice quite their own; close by some young lean, consumptive-looking student, who, cursed with a genius, has come to study at Ri'ad, where he lives on the Coran and the scanty alms of the palace; his head full of true orthodox learning, and his belly empty or nearly so; and others less significant, each on "his business and desire, such as it is," might an Arab Hamlet say.

5

Charles Montagu Doughty
1843-1926

Above:
Charles Montagu Doughty in a portrait by Francis Dodd, c. 1920.

Opposite:
Charles Montagu Doughty's journeys through north-west Arabia and Nejd, 1876-78.

Charles Doughty, tall, red-headed and full-bearded, was one of the more unusual travellers to Saudi Arabia. He was a geologist and linguist, always interested in the scientific aspects of his journeys. When, on his travels, he heard of the ancient desert-city of Medain Salih, more remote and untouched than Petra, he set off dressed as a Syrian, attached to a group of Persians in a caravan heading for Mecca. Towards the end of 1876 he reached Medain Salih, and spent time copying inscriptions on the rock-cut tombs.

His fascination for the nomadic way of life led him to travel for many months with bedouin graziers through their pasture lands and across the volcanic plains to Hail. When he arrived in Hail, in October 1877, he was granted an audience with the Emir and they had a wide-ranging discussion, covering everything from religion to botany. He then travelled south to Khaibar and Unayzah, and thence to Taif with a caravan carrying butter to the Hejaz. More than once during his travels he was robbed and left abandoned in the desert. He nearly died of starvation, was imprisoned, stoned and stripped of all his possessions, and seemed each time to have made a narrow escape, before plunging into further trouble. In August 1878, Doughty entered the British Consulate at Jeddah, and returned to England at the end of that year.

In 1879, he began working on his 600,000-word *Travels in Arabia Deserta*, published nine years later. The book is remarkable for its detailed account of day-to-day bedouin life and for its language, infused with archaic vocabulary, new words and medieval syntax. He told his publisher that he would rather leave it unpublished than change a single word. The result is a unique account of the desert, one which T.E. Lawrence later described as "a book not like other books, but something particular, a bible of its kind."

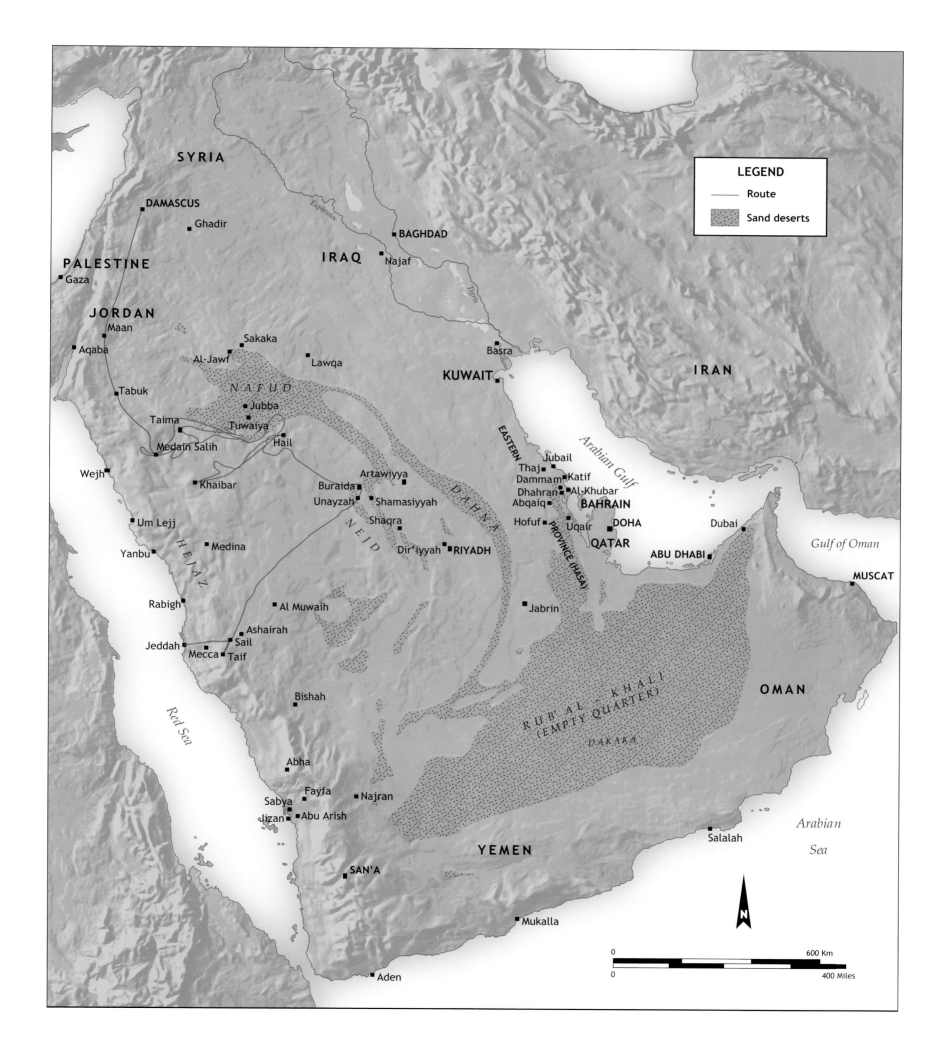

SYRIA

DAMASCUS
Ghadir

PALESTINE

Gaza

JORDAN

Maan

Aqaba

Tabuk

Taima

Medain Salih

Wejh

Um Lejj

Medina

Yanbu

HEJAZ

Rabigh

Ashairah
Sail
Jeddah
Mecca   Taif

Bishah

Abha

Fayfa
Sabya   Najran
Jizan   Abu Arish

SAN'A

Aden

Red Sea

Al-Jawf
Sakaka
Lawqa

NAFUD

Jubba

Tuwaiya
Hail

Khaibar

Buraida
Unayzah
Shamasiyyah
Shaqra

Artawiyya

NEJD

Dir'iyyah   RIYADH

Al Muwaih

YEMEN

Mukalla

Euphrates

IRAQ

BAGHDAD
Najaf

Tigris

Basra

KUWAIT

EASTERN

Thaj
Jubail
Dammam   Katif
Dhahran   Al-Khubar
Abqaiq
Hofuf

PROVINCE (HASA)

DAHNA

Uqair
DOHA
QATAR

BAHRAIN

ABU DHABI

Jabrin

RUB' AL - KHALI
(EMPTY QUARTER)

DAKAKA

Arabian Gulf

IRAN

Gulf of Oman

Dubai

MUSCAT

OMAN

Arabian
Sea

Salalah

LEGEND
— Route
Sand deserts

0 _____ 600 Km
0 _____ 400 Miles

N

Extracts from C. M. Doughty's
Travels in Arabia Deserta

This extract describes Doughty's journey as the only self-confessed Nasrany, or Christian, in a company of 6,000 Muslim pilgrims travelling by camel caravan to Mecca in the autumn of 1876:

The new dawn appearing we removed not yet. The day risen the tents were dismantled, the camels led in ready to their companies, and halted beside their loads. We waited to hear the cannon shot which should open that year's pilgrimage. It was near ten o'clock when we heard the signal gun fired, and then, without any disorder litters were suddenly heaved and braced upon the bearing beasts, their charges laid upon the kneeling camels, and the thousands of riders, all born in the caravan countries, mounted in silence. As all is up, the drivers are left standing upon their feet, or sit to rest out the latest moments on their heels: they with other camp and tent servants must ride those three hundred leagues upon their bare soles, although they faint; and are to measure the ground again upward with their weary feet from the holy places …

It is their caravan prudence, that in the beginning of a long way the first shall be a short journey: the beasts feel their burdens, the passengers have fallen in that to their riding in the field. Of a few sticks (gathered hastily by the way), of the desert bushes, cooking fires are soon kindled before all the tents; and since here are no stones at hand to set under the pots as Beduins use, the pilgrim hearth is a scraped-out hole, so that their vessels may stand, with the brands put under, upon the two brinks, and with very little fuel they make ready their poor messes …

In the first evening hour there is some merrymake of drum-beating and soft fluting, and Arcadian sweetness of the Persians singing in the tents about us; in others they chant together some piece of their devotion. In all the pilgrims' lodgings are paper lanterns with candle burning; but the camp is weary and all is soon at rest. The hajjies lie down in their clothes the few night hours till the morrow gun-fire; then to rise suddenly for the march, and not knowing how early they may hear it, but this is as the rest, after the Pasha's good pleasure and the weather …

Later, Doughty describes entering the sand-desert of Qasim, climbing a high dune, and catching his first glimpse of Buraida:

And from hence appeared a dream-like spectacle! – a great clay town built in this waste sand with enclosing walls and towers and streets and houses! And there beside a bluish dark wood of ethel trees, upon high dunes! This is Boreyda! And that square minaret, in the town, is of the great mesjid. I saw, as it were, Jerusalem in the desert!

On the phenomenon of disease, as spread at that time by pilgrim travellers:

It was now ascertained that the Haj brought the small-pox among them. This terrible disease and cholera-fever are the destruction of nomad Arabia. In their weakly nourished bodies is only little resistance to any malignant sickness. The pilgrimage caravans, (many from the provinces of Arabia herself,) are as torrents of the cities' infection flowing every year through the waste peninsula.

On nourishment during the desert crossings:

We had brought dough tied in a cloth, to spare our water; it had been kneaded at el-Hejr. Of this dough, one made large flat cakes (abud) which, raked under the red-hot sand and embers of our earth, are after a few minutes to be turned. Our bread taken up half baked was crumbled with dates in the hollow of a skin pressed in the sand troughwise, with a little water, that we might feel the less need to drink and make not too soon an end of our little girby, being five persons. The nomads in this country after dates rub their palms in sand; some ruder choughs wipe the cloyed fingers in their long elf locks.

While Doughty had much to praise in the societies he came to know so well, he was frank on the shortcomings of the Bedouin's education:

It is an art to examine the Beduins, of these countries; pains which I took the more willingly, that my passing life might add somewhat of lasting worth to the European geography. Of the Peninsula of the Arabs, large nearly as India, we have been in ignorance more than of any considerable country in the world which remains to be visited. There are difficulties in these enquiries; the rudeness of the common sort of minds, and the few sheykhly men who are of a better understanding, dwelling all the days of their destitute lives in the tent shadows, are those that have least topical knowledge. The short levity of the most will glance from your question, they think thy asking vain, and they think thee fond. – You shall have also their wily crooked answers, yielded with little willingness by these free-born wretches, jealous of their wandering grounds and waters.

Lady Anne Blunt

1837-1917

Above:
Lady Anne Blunt in Arab dress, 1907.

Opposite:
Lady Anne Blunt's journey to Hail, 1879.

Lady Anne Blunt was the first western woman to cross the Nafud desert and the first to visit the town of Hail in Nejd, central Arabia. She and her husband, Wilfrid Scawen Blunt, went there in search of the thoroughbred Arab horse.

Lady Anne was the granddaughter of Lord Byron. An unconventional upbringing was followed by an adventurous married life: she and Wilfrid made several excursions into the Syrian and Arabian deserts. Their most daring expedition was a journey to Nejd, the homeland of the Arabian horse, in 1879. They covered 400 miles of stony desert between Damascus and Al-Jawf. On the way they were ambushed in a ghazzu, or raid, by bedouin. At Al-Jawf they were told the route to Hail was quite safe as "all persons found away from the high road have their heads cut off". They crossed the great red Nafud desert to Hail, where they called upon the Emir, who, although notorious for his cruelty, treated them with kindness. "Hail was a lion's den, though fortunately we were friends with the lion", wrote Lady Anne.

She recorded their travels and adventures in diaries and watercolours, and wrote two books to which Wilfrid contributed some chapters: *A Pilgrimage to Nejd* and *Bedouin Tribes of the Euphrates*. Wilfrid, born in 1840, was deemed "too handsome to live" by one of his many female admirers. A poet, sometime diplomat and diarist, he became embroiled in many revolutionary causes and wrote prolifically on a variety of political subjects. Although their marriage was ultimately not a happy one owing to Wilfrid's philandering, through the foundation of the Crabbet Stud in Sussex and the Sheykh Obeyd Stud in Cairo, they preserved the true thoroughbred Arabian horse from extinction. Lady Anne died alone in Cairo in 1917.

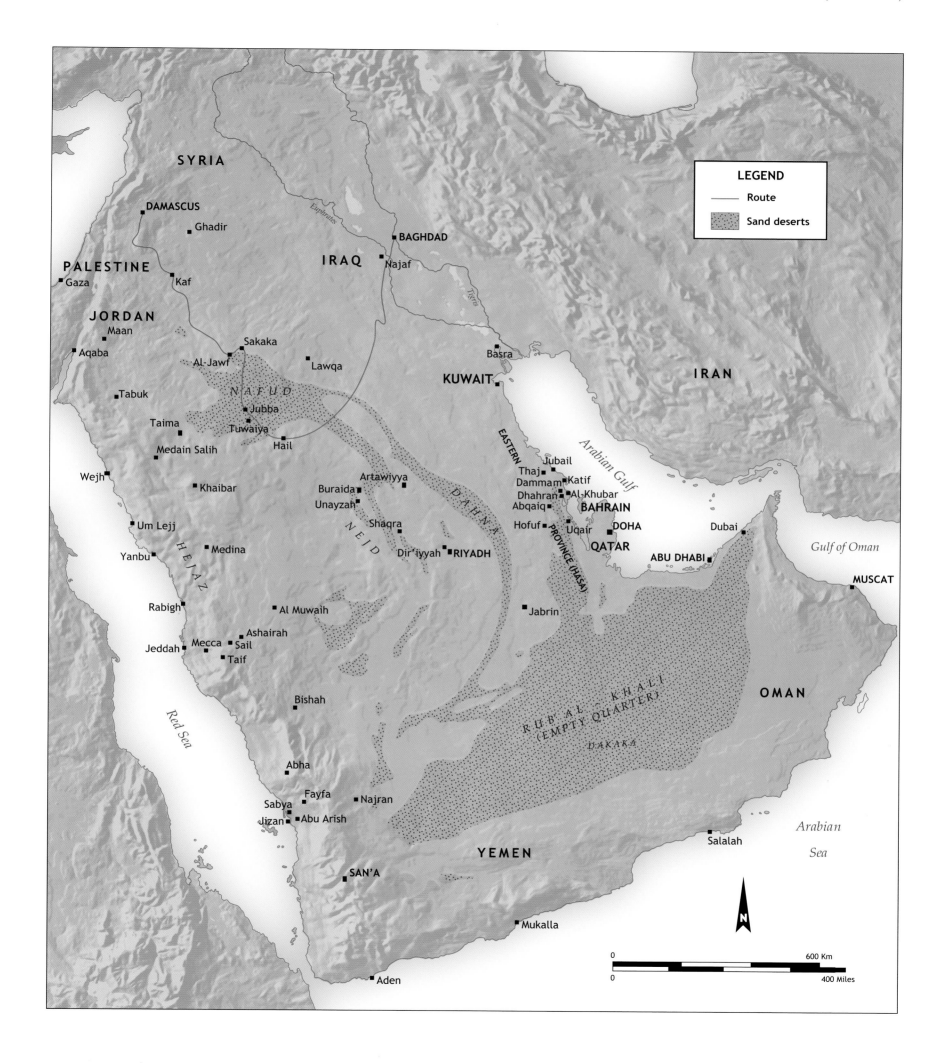

SYRIA

DAMASCUS
Ghadir

PALESTINE

Gaza

JORDAN

Maan

Aqaba

Kaf

Tabuk

Taima

Medain Salih

Wejh

Um Lejj

Yanbu

Rabigh

Jeddah
Mecca
Sail
Taif
Ashairah

HEJAZ

Medina

Al Muwaih

Bishah

Abha

Sabya
Jizan
Fayfa
Abu Arish

Najran

SAN'A

Aden

Euphrates

IRAQ
Najaf

BAGHDAD

Tigris

Sakaka
Al-Jawf
Lawqa

NAFUD
Jubba
Tuwaiya
Hail

Khaibar

Buraida
Unayzah

Artawiyya

Shaqra

NEJD

Dir'iyyah   RIYADH

Basra

KUWAIT

EASTERN

Jubail
Thaj
Dammam
Dhahran
Abqaiq
Hofuf

Katif
Al-Khubar

BAHRAIN

Uqair
DOHA
QATAR

Arabian Gulf

IRAN

Dubai

ABU DHABI

Gulf of Oman

MUSCAT

PROVINCE (HASA)

DAHNA

Jabrin

RUB' AL KHALI
(EMPTY QUARTER)

DAKAKA

OMAN

Salalah

Arabian
Sea

YEMEN

Mukalla

Red Sea

LEGEND

Route

Sand deserts

N

| 0 | | 600 Km |
| 0 | | 400 Miles |

Jubba, men outside gateway   *January 1879*

Watercolour sketch

After crossing the great red sand-dunes of the Nafud desert in northern Arabia, the Blunts approached Jubba on their way to visit the Emir of Hail, in late January 1879. Lady Anne wrote: "It was nearly sunset when we first saw Jobba itself, below us at the edge of the subkha (dried-up lakebed), with dark green palms cutting the pale blue of the dry lake and beyond that a group of red rocks rising out of the pink Nafud: in the foreground yellow sand tufted with adr; the whole scene transfigured by the evening light and beautiful beyond description. Jobba is one of the most curious places in the world and to my mind one of the most beautiful. Its name Jobba, or rather Jubbeh, meaning a well, explains its position, for it lies in a hole or well in the Nafud … The village is extremely picturesque, with its little battlemented walls and its gardens."

Palm groves of Agde, Jebel Shammar   *January 1879*

Watercolour sketch

Hail is surrounded by the mountains of the Jebel Shammar, strikingly beautiful scenery which appealed greatly to Lady Anne. She wrote in her journal as she sat looking at the mountains before her: "It is like a dream to be sitting here, writing a journal on a rock in Jebel Shammar." Later, in her book A Pilgrimage to Nejd, she wrote: "The view in front of us was beautiful beyond description, a perfectly even plain, sloping gradually upwards, out of which these rocks and tells cropped up like islands and beyond it the violet-coloured mountains now close before us … The outline of Jebel Shammar is strangely fantastic, running up into spires and domes and pinnacles, with here and there a loop-hole through which you can see the sky, or a wonderful boulder perched like a rocking stone on the sky line."

House at Hail   *January 1879*

Watercolour sketch

The Blunts reached Hail on 24 January 1879. They were courteously welcomed by the
Emir of Hail, Muhammad ibn Rashid, who provided them with a house in the main street
of Hail. Anne described it as "a house without pretence, but sufficient for our wants, and
secure from all intruders, for the street door could be locked and the walls were high. It
consisted of two separate houses, as I believe most dwellings in Arabia do, one for men and
the other for women ... [the latter] had a small open court, just large enough for the three
mares to stand in, an open vestibule ... and two little dens ... All was exceedingly simple
but in decent repair and clean, the only ornaments being certain patterns scratched out in
white from the brown wash which covered the walls."

Pilgrim column leaving Hail   *February 1879*

Watercolour sketch

After almost a week in Hail, the Blunts made plans to travel on to Baghdad. They attached themselves to a caravan of Persian pilgrims returning home from Mecca. The caravan followed the ancient pilgrim road from Najaf to Medina and Mecca, known as the Darb Zubeidah. The procession which the Blunts joined had within it 4,000 camels and even more people, and was three miles long. It took them five weeks to cover the 600 miles from Hail to Baghdad.

Captain William Shakespear C.I.E.

1878-1915

Above:
Captain Shakespear in a portrait from the Geographical Journal, *1922.*

Opposite:
Captain Shakespear's trans-Arabian route, 1914.

The twin achievements of Captain William Shakespear's short life were to map and record uncharted areas of the north of Arabia, and to establish a lasting bond of trust with King Abdul-Aziz Ibn Saud. Shakespear was born in India and educated in England. In 1899 he joined the Bengal Lancers and quickly became fluent in Urdu, Pushtu, Farsi and Arabic. In 1904 he entered the diplomatic sphere, becoming the youngest consul in the Indian administration. In 1909 he became Political Agent in Kuwait and from there made seven expeditions by camel into Eastern and Central Arabia. In 1910 he met Ibn Saud, Emir of Nejd and the future king of Saudi Arabia, and the two struck up a lasting friendship.

Shakespear's greatest journey was undertaken in 1914, when he crossed Arabia from Kuwait to Suez via Riyadh, some 1,800 miles in all; two-thirds of it through uncharted territory. Shakespear made meticulous notes, took altitude and barometer readings, photographed and mapped his routes through the Peninsula. His command of Nejdi Arabic enabled him to gain vital local knowledge.

At the outbreak of the First World War Shakespear was appointed Britain's official representative to Ibn Saud. Early in 1915 he accompanied the Emir as he moved north to face the forces of the ruler of Hail, and insisted on taking part in the ensuing Battle of Jarrab. Before the fighting began, Ibn Saud asked his friend to retreat to safety. Shakespear replied, "I have been ordered to be with you. If I leave now it would be a blemish to my honour, and the honour of my country. Therefore excuse me. I must certainly be with you." As battle commenced, he stationed himself alone on rising ground to observe the enemy army, and was shot and killed.

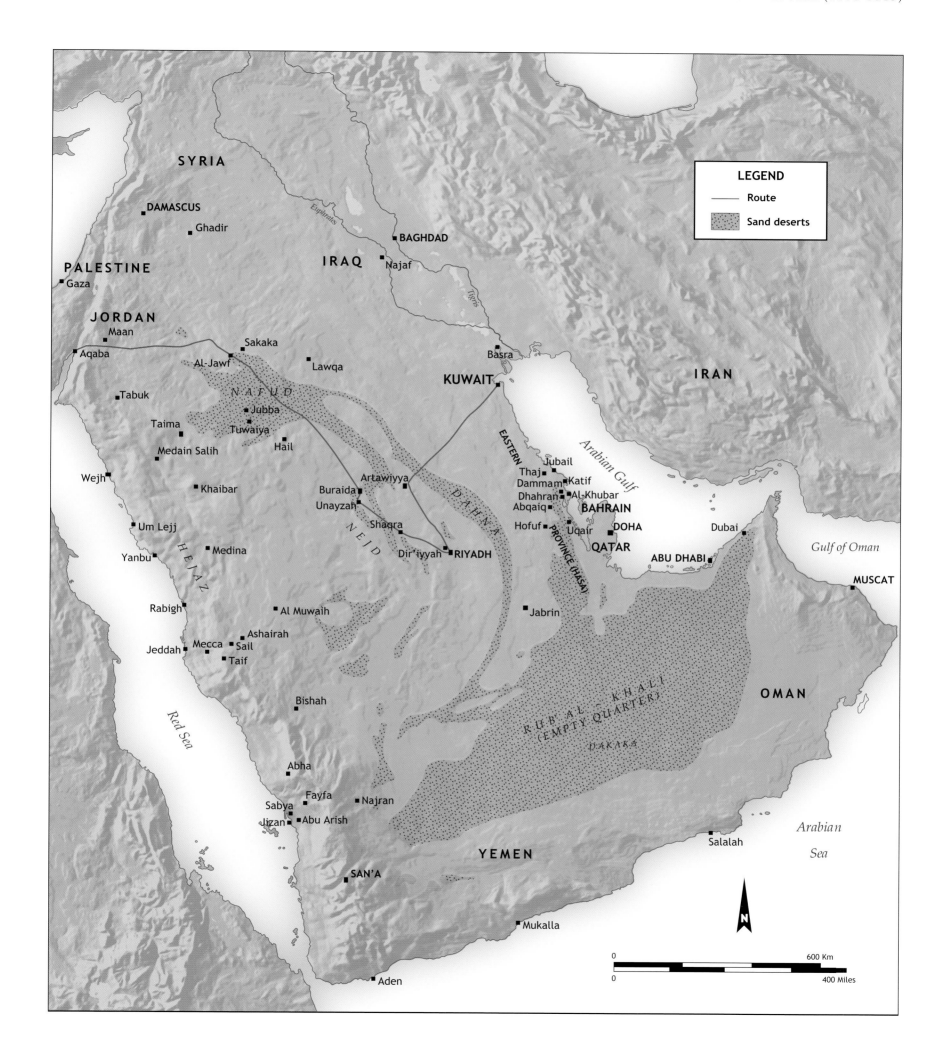

A newborn camel carried by its mother in a saddlebag, As-Safa

February 1910

Shakespear made seven desert journeys while he was stationed in Kuwait as Political Agent from 1909 to 1914. On this, his second journey, he ventured to As-Safa in the north-eastern reaches of Nejd, surveying the uncharted territory across the Subhan desert and beyond. On the way, Shakespear's camp was attacked by bandits, and his chief guide, Khalaq, fatally shot.

Ibn Saud and Shaikh Mubarak of Kuwait with members of the Al Saud family and retainers, Kuwait *February 1910*

Shakespear was first introduced to Emir, later King, Abdul-Aziz Ibn Saud in Kuwait. The two struck up an almost instant friendship, the former describing Ibn Saud as "fair, handsome and … after initial reserve, of genial and courteous manner." Ibn Saud readily agreed to be photographed, and this is one of the earliest known photographs of him. Ibn Saud is seated in the centre-left of the picture, holding prayer beads. Shaikh Mubarak of Kuwait sits next to him.

Ibn Saud, his brothers and his elder sons at camp near Thaj
March 1911

In February 1911 Shakespear set off to explore and map the remote region bounded by the Hasa oasis and the great Dahna sandbelt. In this remote region he found Ibn Saud at camp with his brothers and elder sons. For three days, the two men hunted together and talked long into the night, cementing their close friendship. In this photograph, Ibn Saud is seated, centre. Standing behind him on the left, with two long plaits, is his brother Sa'd ibn Abd al-Rahman, who was killed at Kinzan just four years later, in 1915.

The main street of Riyadh   *March 1914*

Shakespear's seventh and final desert journey, begun after he had finished as Political Agent in Kuwait, took him across the Nafud desert and down to Ibn Saud's capital, Riyadh. He wrote of his meeting: "Taken through the east gate along a wide road, past … some big houses built on a palatial scale. Greeted warmly by Abdul-Aziz and Sa'd." During the three days of his stay, he was able to roam around the town and take photographs.

**Distribution of camels before a raid,
Shamsiyyah Gardens, Riyadh**   *March 1914*

Abdul-Aziz invited Shakespear to ride out of Riyadh with him at the start of a raid.
Shakespear observed the preparations for the military expedition and discovered that he
was to march with the standard party – a unique experience for a westerner. After two days
he left the expedition and continued on his own trans-Arabian crossing. Less than a year
later Shakespear was killed whilst observing the battle at Jarrab between Ibn Saud's forces
and the Rashidis of Hail.

Following pages:

Ibn Saud's army on the march   *1914*

This photograph shows Ibn Saud's *hamla*, or military expedition, leaving Riyadh in March 1914. Shakespear wrote that the standard was "green with the kalima (maxim) on it in white." As it appears on the Saudi Arabian national flag today, the kalima was: "There is no God but Allah and Muhammad is the Prophet of Allah."

Gertrude Bell C.B.E.
1868-1926

Above:
Gertrude Bell, 1921.

Opposite:
Gertrude Bell's journey to Hail, 1914.

Gertrude Bell was born in Washington, Co. Durham of wealthy industrialist parents. She was, from an early age, outstanding: one of the first women to get a First in history from Oxford, an accomplished linguist and a mountaineer of great renown. From the final years of the 19th century onwards, her life became increasingly governed by a love of travel, and of the Persian and Arab world. She learned Arabic, Farsi and Turkish, investigated many archaeological sites, published translations of Persian poetry and wrote several travel books.

In 1914, Gertrude bought 20 camels in Damascus, and left with five local guides for the isolated city of Hail. She travelled down through Amman and the Jordanian desert, approaching the Nafud desert from the north-west. When she arrived at Hail she was entertained by members of the ruling family, but informed that she would not be allowed to leave her guest-house. Only on the last morning was she permitted to stroll in the town and take photographs.

Gertrude's knowledge of Arabia and its tribes was noted by British Intelligence. During the First World War she worked for the Arab Bureau, and was appointed Oriental Secretary to the High Commissioner, Sir Percy Cox, in Baghdad. In November 1916 she became the first European woman to meet the future King Abdul-Aziz, acting as his escort during his visit to Basra.

In 1921 Winston Churchill led a group of Middle East experts to the Cairo Conference to discuss the future of Mesopotamia, and Gertrude Bell was among the delegates. Her role in helping to determine the borders of Iraq, and advising its first ruler, King Faisal, earned her renown in Iraq, where she was known as 'Al Khatun' or 'Lady of the Court'. She died in Baghdad in 1926.

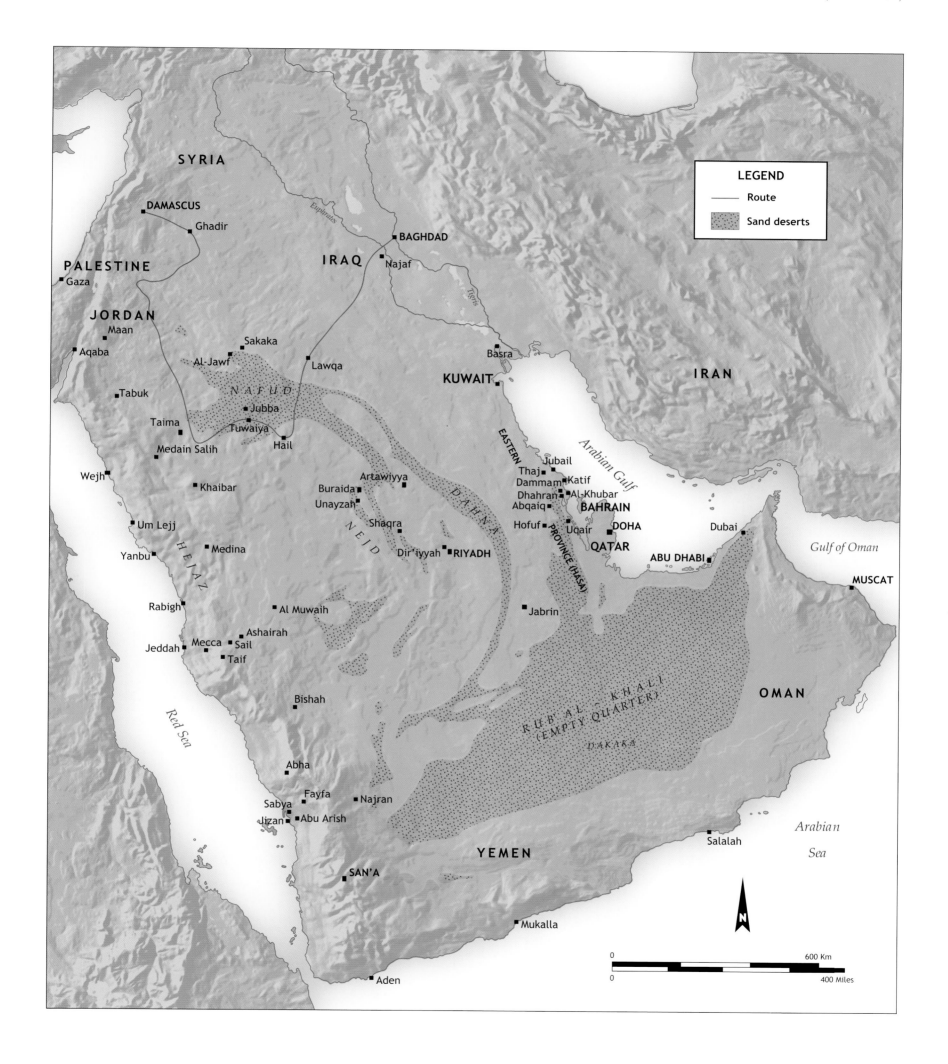

SYRIA

DAMASCUS

Ghadir

Euphrates

BAGHDAD

IRAQ

Najaf

PALESTINE

Gaza

JORDAN

Maan

Aqaba

Sakaka

Al-Jawf

Lawqa

Basra

Tigris

KUWAIT

IRAN

Tabuk

N A F U D

Jubba

Taima

Tuwaiya

Medain Salih

Hail

EASTERN

Wejh

Khaibar

Artawiyya

D A H N A

Jubail

Arabian Gulf

Buraida

Thaj

Katif

Unayzah

Dammam

Al-Khubar

Dhahran

Um Lejj

N E J D

Shaqra

Abqaiq

BAHRAIN

H E J A Z

Medina

Dir'iyyah

RIYADH

Hofuf

Uqair

DOHA

Yanbu

PROVINCE (HASA)

QATAR

Dubai

ABU DHABI

Rabigh

Al Muwaih

Jabrin

MUSCAT

Gulf of Oman

Mecca

Ashairah

Jeddah

Sail

Taif

OMAN

Bishah

R U B' A L - K H A L I
(EMPTY QUARTER)

D A K A K A

Abha

Fayfa

Sabya

Najran

Jizan

Abu Arish

Red Sea

YEMEN

Salalah

*Arabian
Sea*

Mukalla

SAN'A

N

Aden

0   600 Km

0   400 Miles

Muhammad abu Tayyih's tent, Howeitat territory
January 1914

Gertrude Bell had been travelling for six weeks when she and her caravan arrived in Howeitat territory, at Tor At-Tubaiq. She was entertained by Muhammad abu Tayyih, the brother of Shaikh Auda, the great Howeitat chief who played such a vital role in the Arab Revolt alongside T.E. Lawrence. She also met many other members of the tribe and their womenfolk.

Camp in Nafud   *February/March 1914*

Gertrude described travelling in the Nafud desert: "Marching through the Nafud is like marching through the Labyrinth. You are forever winding round deep sand pits, sometimes half a mile long, with banks so steep that you cannot descend. They are mostly shaped like horseshoes and you wander along until you come to the end and then drop down into low ground, only to climb up anew."

Following pages:

Outside the mosque, Hail   *February 1914*

On 25 February, Gertrude entered Hail. She wrote: "Hail as it stands is of comparatively recent date, but it preserves a traditional architecture which goes back, I make no doubt, to very early times." She was especially struck by the call to prayer which woke her every morning: "'Allahu akbar, Allahu akbar – God is great, God is great' ... Low and soft, borne on the scented breeze of the desert, the mighty invocation, which is the Alpha and Omega of Islam, sounds through my memory when I think of Hail."

Above:

The battlemented walls of Hail   *March 1914*

Before Gertrude left Hail, she was allowed to take photographs of the town. She wrote eloquent descriptions of the "silent ways paved with desert dust", and "the battlemented ring of mud wall [which] encircles Hail, the line broken at regular intervals by ruined towers, battlemented also, machicolated, narrowing upwards like wingless windmills."

Opposite:

Roshan, or reception room, at the Rashid summer palace in Hail *February 1914*

Gertrude was led into the summer palace of the Rashids, the powerful rulers of Hail. She described the reception room, or Roshan, in which she was entertained, as "a great room with a roof borne on columns and divans and carpets around the walls." After lunch, Ibrahim ibn Rashid, the Emir's deputy, paid her a visit. "He was clothed in Indian silks and carried a gold-mounted sword," she wrote.

35

T.E. Lawrence
1888-1935

Above:
T.E. Lawrence in Arab head-dress, 1917.

Opposite:
The framed section shows a representation of Map III in Lawrence's
Seven Pillars of Wisdom, *showing his routes between Jeddah and*
Aqaba during the Arab Revolt.

Colonel T.E. Lawrence, better known as 'Lawrence of Arabia', is most famous for the role he played in organising the revolt of the Arabs of the Hejaz against their Ottoman overlords during the First World War. In 1916 he first met Emir Faisal bin Hussain. "I felt at first glance," he wrote, "this was the man I had come to Arabia to seek — the leader who would bring the Arab Revolt to full glory." Faisal's army mounted a prolonged period of guerilla warfare against the Ottomans, repeatedly attacking the Turks' main means of communication, the Hejaz Railway.

In April 1917, Faisal was joined by Auda abu Tayyi, the powerful leader of the Howeitat tribe. Three months later, Lawrence accompanied Auda on an expedition sent by Faisal to raise the northern tribes, resulting in the capture of the Turkish-held coastal base of Aqaba.

Lawrence wrote about this campaign in *Seven Pillars of Wisdom.* Subtitled 'A Triumph', and published in 1926, it chronicles the constant raiding parties and described what it was to live as a bedouin in the desert. It was a life Lawrence greatly admired. He realised that in order to lead his men in battle, he would have to live as they did. "The Arabs," he wrote, "taught me that no man could be their leader except he ate the ranks' food, wore their clothes, lived level with them, and yet appeared better in himself."

Lawrence's achievements in Arabia were prodigious: his two-month journey over more than one thousand miles of desert, ending in the capture of the key coastal position of Aqaba, and his crossing of the Sinai in a 49-hour camel ride, have become the stuff of legend, thanks in part to the lyricism of his writing and the many photographs he took.

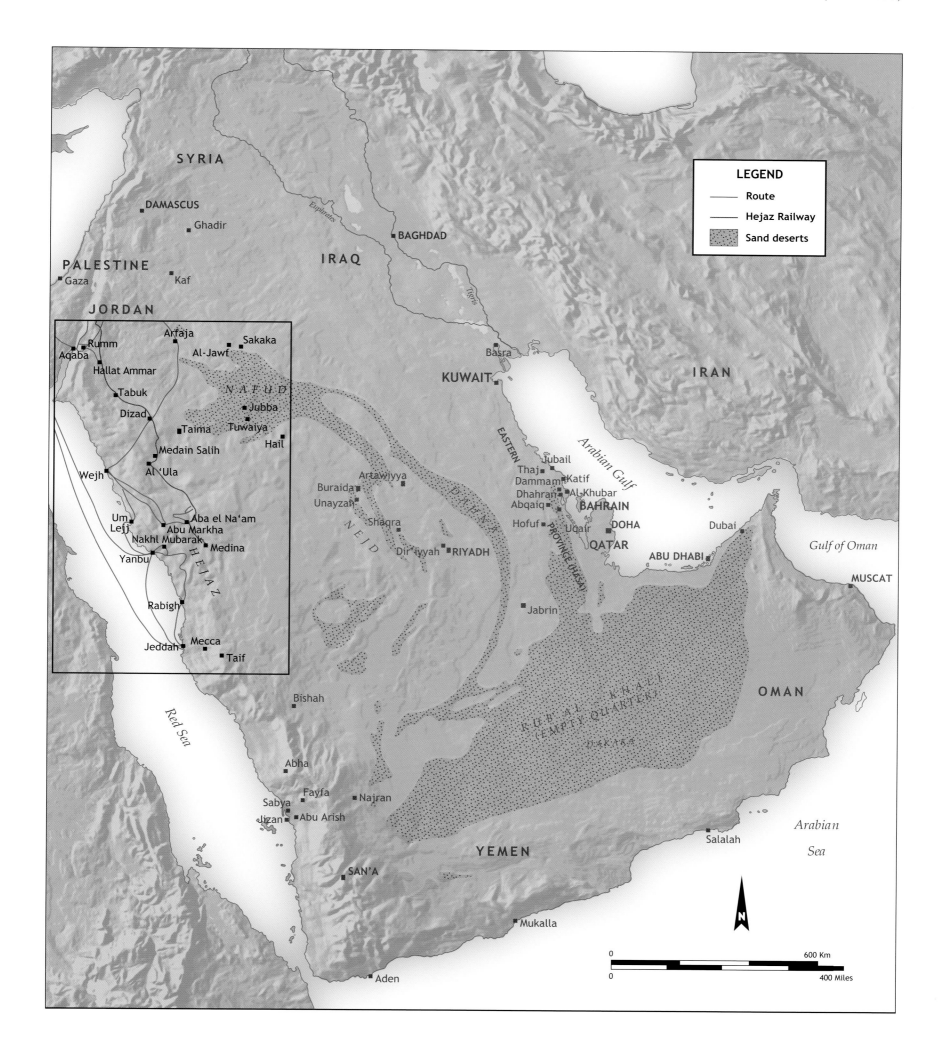

Yanbu, with the house where Lawrence stayed on the right
November 1916

In November 1916 Lawrence returned to the Hejaz to rejoin Faisal, who was in Yanbu An-Nakhl, just off the coastal plain. At Yanbu, "the second sea-port of Hejaz", Lawrence stayed with Abdel Qadir, Faisal's agent, "in his picturesque rambling house looking over the deserted square, whence so many Medina caravans had started." At this stage, Yanbu was the special base of Faisal's army. Several of Lawrence's compatriots were teaching the Arabs how to blow up railways with dynamite, and how to keep army stores in order. Lawrence found the atmosphere among the Arab fighters at Yanbu "busy and confident".

Scene in camp at dawn, Nakhl Mubarak
December 1916

Lawrence, Faisal and the Arab army camped at Nakhl Mubarak for two days in December 1916, and Lawrence spent a great deal of time with Faisal, observing with admiration his leadership and character. "The routine of our life in camp was simple," he wrote. "Just before daybreak, the army Imam used to climb to the head of the little hill above the sleeping army and thence utter an astounding call to prayer ... we were effectively roused ... In a minute one of Faisal's five slaves came round ... with sweetened coffee. Sugar for the first cup in the chill of dawn was considered fit."

Above:

Faisal's army coming into Wejh   *January 1917*

By the time the Arab army arrived at the outskirts of Wejh, the Royal Navy had already attacked and overwhelmed the Turkish troops, and naval seamen and Arabs were occupying the town. Faisal's army marched towards Wejh cautiously, uncertain of the situation. Lawrence wrote: "They advanced by alternate companies, in open order, at intervals of four or five yards, with even-numbered companies in support, making good use of the poor cover which existed … they went along in a steady lope … dead silent, and reached and climbed the ridge without a shot fired. So we knew the work had been finished for us." This was the moment, Lawrence later reflected, "that the Hejaz war was won".

Opposite:

Um Lejj   *January 1917*

Faisal and Lawrence moved the army north to the coastal settlement of Wejh. On their way they stopped at Um Lejj. Lawrence had been taken there by ship, and he and his compatriot Boyle examined the town, which had been badly shelled by Boyle himself, from his ship the Fox, a few months earlier. At Um Lejj, Lawrence and Faisal drew up a timetable and plan of attack for the crucial entry into Wejh.

Above:

General view of Medina   *1916-18*

Lawrence did not go to Medina during the war, but this photograph, which forms part of
the T.E. Lawrence Collection in the Imperial War Museum, shows a view of Medina as it
was during the Arab Revolt. Medina had strong fortifications, and was defended by 14,000
well-equipped regular Turkish troops. It was also the southernmost terminal of the Hejaz
Railway. With the capture of the port town of Wejh in January 1917, the Turks could no
longer threaten Mecca, and were effectively pinned down to Medina and the garrison posts
of the railway. They would remain there for the rest of the war.

Right:

Railway track near Abu Taka   *1917*

After the capture of Wejh, the Arabs and their British allies began their attacks on the
Hejaz Railway in earnest. The aim was, in Lawrence's words, "to keep his [the Turk's]
railway just working, but only just, with the maximum of loss and discomfort." This
meant blowing up trains and sections of track, diverting troops and resources into making
costly repairs, and hindering the transportation of men, food and equipment. "Mines were
the best weapon yet discovered to make the regular working of their trains costly and
uncertain for our Turkish enemy," wrote Lawrence.

Previous pages:

Arab camp at Wejh   *February 1917*

"Life in Wejh was interesting," wrote Lawrence. The army had set their camp in order,
Faisal had pitched his tents, "living tents, reception tents, staff tents, guest tents, servants'"
about a mile from the sea. "The tents of soldiers and tribesmen were grouped in these
sandy valleys, leaving the chill height for ourselves; and very delightful in the evening we
northerners found it when the breeze from the sea carried us a murmur of the waves …
Immediately beneath us were the Ageyl, an irregular close group of tents … further out
the market was set plainly on the ground." The scattered tents and shelters of the
tribesmen were set in every gully, and "beyond the last of them lay open country."

Lt-Col G. Leachman D.S.O.

1880-1920

Lt-Colonel Leachman was commissioned into the Royal Sussex Regiment, and served in the Boer War and in India. He made his first expedition into Arabia in 1909, during which he was caught up in a raid by the Anaiza tribe against the Shammar near Hail. Leachman wrote a vivid eye-witness account of the two tribes in battle.

In 1912 he embarked on a second expedition into Saudi Arabia, with the aim of crossing the Empty Quarter (the Rub' Al-Khali). He left from Damascus, crossed the Nafud desert to Al-Qassim, and from there made his way to Riyadh. Leachman was the first Briton to be received by Ibn Saud in his home city. He was well treated, although he was not permitted to enter the Empty Quarter, and instead travelled east to Hasa.

He subsequently spent several years as a political officer in Iraq and was murdered near Fallujah on 12 August 1920. Gertrude Bell said of Leachman: "He was a wild soldier of fortune, but a very gallant officer and his name was known all over Arabia."

Above:
Lt-Col G. Leachman in 1912.

On the outskirts of the Nafud desert *1912*

Leachman left Damascus for Riyadh on 3 November 1912, accompanied by a companion
from his previous journey, an Arab named Saleh Mutaweh, and two tribesmen from
Qasim. He was travelling to Riyadh, and afterwards hoped to obtain permission from
Emir Abdul-Aziz Ibn Saud to enter the Rub' Al-Khali or Empty Quarter. His journey took
him through the Nafud desert.

Ayun al-Jawa, in the Qasim region *1912*

Ayun lies on the road from Hail to Buraida. It was a town of some 4,000 inhabitants when Leachman passed through. His companion Saleh, it turned out, was the brother of the Emir of Ayun, and Leachman and his companions were treated to a feast in their honour. He found the inhabitants "broad-minded, business-like and travelled, and the community a happy one."

The ruined city of Dir'iyyah   *1912*

On his way to Riyadh, Leachman passed the ruins of Dir'iyyah, the once-great capital of the first Saudi state and the centre of an empire that flourished between 1745 and 1818. The city, which dominated the peninsula and its holy places, was sacked by the Egyptians under Ibrahim Pasha in 1818.

Following pages:
The Hasa [Thumayri] Gate at Riyadh   *1912*

Leachman stayed in Riyadh for a week, as the honoured guest of Emir Abdul-Aziz. When asked by an old man why he was entertaining a Christian in such style, Abdul-Aziz replied, "any Englishman, whether Christian or not, is my friend." The two men enjoyed long conversations about current world events, and Leachman left with a favourable impression of the Emir, even though he was denied permission to enter the Empty Quarter. He headed instead for Hofuf, which was still garrisoned by the Turks, and thence to Bahrain.

Major R.E. Cheesman C.B.E.

1878-1962

Major R.E. Cheesman was a military officer with an interest in nature, particularly bird watching. He spent many years in Arabia on recording expeditions. During a journey to Saudi Arabia in late 1923, he collected more than 300 specimens of wildlife from the Hasa oasis, which he subsequently donated to the British Museum. Several of the species he collected from Arabia were previously unknown to science.

Early in his journey, Cheesman was invited to present his findings to Ibn Saud at his court in Hofuf. He later recalled his pleasure at finding the future king so knowledgeable about the local wildlife. After Hofuf, Cheesman travelled south and was the first European to visit Jabrin on the northern fringes of the Empty Quarter.

Above:
Major R.E. Cheesman

Left:
The colonnade of the Qaysariyyah, Hofuf   *1923*

The Suq Al-Khamis, or Thursday market, was the hub of commercial life in Hofuf, and was famed throughout eastern Arabia for its local and imported goods. This distinctive and elegant colonnaded section of the suq, the Qaysariyyah, housed a permanent, covered section of the market.

Previous pages:
Walls of the Royal palace, Hofuf   *1923*

Hofuf, traditionally the chief town of inland eastern Arabia, acted as the administrative centre of the Eastern Province until 1953. The old town was divided into three quarters, Kut, Rifa'ah and Na'athil. The Royal palace was located in the Kut quarter, in the north-west of the city.

Major A.L. Holt M.B.E., M.C.

1896-1971

In the early 1920s Major A.L. Holt of the Royal Engineers undertook a series of journeys through Arabia in order to assess the possibility of constructing a trans-desert railway. On one occasion he travelled with Lt-Colonel Leachman, and on another he was accompanied by H. St. J. B. Philby to the Jawf region. Holt travelled some 14,000 miles through the desert, and many of his journeys were undertaken in Ford cars. In a detailed report to the Royal Geographical Society, delivered in 1923, he outlined his proposed railway route, and the advantages of travelling by car instead of camels: "I have taken a convoy of Fords 350 miles in the desert without touching water," he wrote. "The extraordinary advantage of this in reconnaissance needs no emphasis." Despite Holt's enthusiasm for the project however, the trans-desert railway was never built.

Unfortunately no portrait of Holt exists today.

Opposite above:
Camel litters for transport of women, Kaf   *1922*

The women's camel litter, or hawdaj, was covered with cloth to shade women and children from the sun while on the move through the punishing heat of the desert. While Holt recognised that camels enabled a traveller to reach areas that were impassable for a car, he saw the camel as unsuitable for his reconnaissance requirements, because camel watering-places often required deviation from the most direct route.

Opposite below:
Qasr Marid, Dumat al-Jandal, Al-Jawf   *1922*

Holt visited the oasis of Dumat al-Jandal, the old capital of Al-Jawf, as part of a reconnaissance to assess the feasibility of a Baghdad-Aqaba rail link, via Al-Jawf. He was accompanied on this journey by H. St. J. B. Philby, whose mission was to assess the desirability of extending Transjordan's sovereignty to include Al-Jawf. At the time of their visit, Qasr Marid was a stronghold of the nomadic Al Sha'alan shaikhs of the Ruwala tribe. The rest of Al-Jawf was held in Ibn Saud's name.

Above:

Sakaka oasis, Al-Jawf *1922*

Sakaka was an important oasis of Al-Jawf, and it supported several outlying villages. Its waters were still drawn by camels and cows, as they had been since pre-Islamic times. Away from the palm-fringed oasis, the surrounding terrain, Holt reported, "is an undulating, terraced sandstone plain, barren and unproductive."

Previous pages:

Holt's Ford in difficulties *1922*

Holt was one of the earliest travellers by car through the Syrian desert. He regarded the motor-car as the best form of transport for the task of railway reconnaissance, which was his speciality. "In all my desert travelling with the Fords," he wrote, "I have never experienced a mechanical delay of over one and a half hours, and on one occasion I covered more than 170 miles in a single day."

The village and oasis of Kaf *1922*

The oasis of Kaf was one of the Qurayyat Milh or 'Salt Villages' to be found at the northern end of Wadi Sirhan. Holt estimated that some 3,000 to 7,000 tons of salt were sent out of Kaf annually, making it one of the most important exporting settlements in the region. The fort in the bottom right of the picture had recently been built by the Al Sha'alan shaikhs of the Ruwala.

H. St J. B. Philby C.I.E.
1885-1960

Above:
H. St J. B. Philby standing by the mobile wireless station at Hofuf, 1932.

Opposite:
H. St J. B. Philby's crossing of the Rub' Al-Khali, 1932.

Harry St J. B. Philby, a remarkable linguist and polymath, was the second westerner to cross the Rub' Al-Khali, or Empty Quarter. His close friendship with King Abdul-Aziz gave him access to remote areas of the desert, which he not only explored, but mapped and recorded in his many books. His son, Soviet agent Kim Philby, inscribed 'Greatest of Arabian explorers' on his Beirut tombstone.

Philby was born in Ceylon in 1885, and educated at Westminster and Cambridge. He joined the Indian Civil Service in 1907 and was posted to Basra in 1915. Two years later he went on a British mission to Ibn Saud, then Emir of Nejd, and crossed central Arabia from east to west. He was immediately impressed with the future king, later describing him as "a friend beyond all price". The following year Philby travelled from Riyadh to Sulayyil, making the first of many maps.

In 1921 Philby succeeded T.E. Lawrence as Chief British Representative in Transjordan, but from 1925 onwards he spent most of his life in Saudi Arabia. He set up a trading company, and acted as adviser at Ibn Saud's court. He became a Muslim in 1930, and at the King's suggestion took the name Abdullah. In early 1932 he fulfilled his long-held ambition to cross the Empty Quarter, crossing from Jabrin to Sulayyil. In 1936 Philby mapped his journey from Najran to the Hadhramaut and Mukalla, and surveyed the Saudi-Yemeni border for Ibn Saud. In 1950 he travelled 3,000 miles in 98 days to explore the legendary land of Midian, and the following year he led the first archaeological expedition to work under the patronage of Ibn Saud, during which over 12,000 inscriptions were recorded. Philby died in 1960, having explored, mapped and described more of the Arabian Peninsula than any other traveller, and having enriched many museum collections and institutions in the process. He is the author of numerous books on Arabia including *A Pilgrim in Arabia* and *The Empty Quarter.*

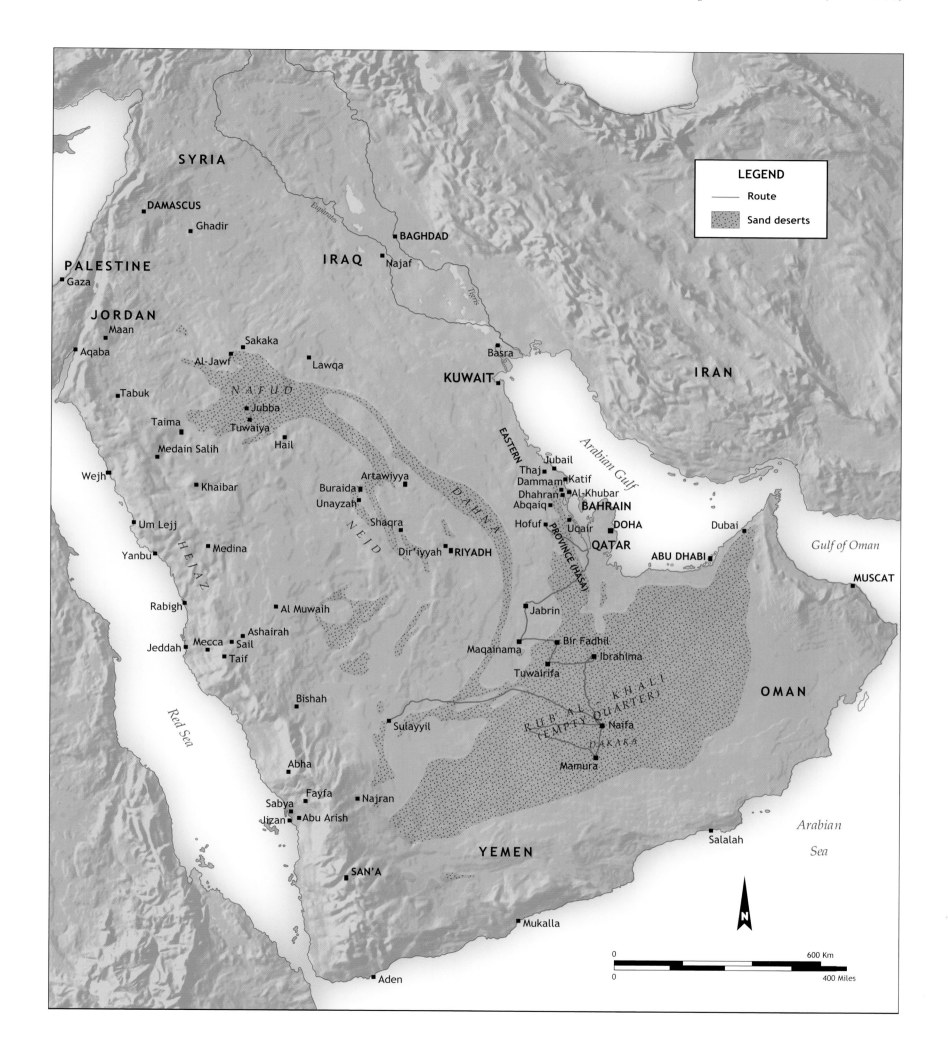

LEGEND

Route

Sand deserts

SYRIA

DAMASCUS

Ghadir

PALESTINE

Gaza

IRAQ

BAGHDAD

Najaf

JORDAN

Maan

Aqaba

Tabuk

Taima

Medain Salih

Wejh

Um Lejj

Yanbu

HEJAZ

Rabigh

Ashairah

Mecca   Sail

Jeddah   Taif

Bishah

Abha

Fayfa   Najran

Sabya

Jizan   Abu Arish

SAN'A

Aden

Sakaka

Al-Jawf   Lawqa

NAFUD

Jubba

Tuwaiya

Hail

Khaibar

Artawiyya

Buraida

Unayzah

Shaqra

Medina

NEJD

Dir'iyyah   RIYADH

Al Muwaih

Sulayyil

Basra

KUWAIT

IRAN

EASTERN

DAHNA

Jubail

Thaj   Dammam

Katif

Dhahran   Al-Khubar

Abqaiq   BAHRAIN

Hofuf   BAHRAIN

PROVINCE (HASA)

Uqair   DOHA

QATAR

ABU DHABI

Dubai

Gulf of Oman

MUSCAT

Jabrin

Maqainama   Bir Fadhil

Ibrahima

Tuwairifa

KHALI

(EMPTY QUARTER)

RUB' AL

Naifa

DAKAKA

Mamura

OMAN

Salalah

Arabian
Sea

YEMEN

Mukalla

Arabian Gulf

Euphrates

Tigris

Red Sea

N

0   600 Km

0   400 Miles

63

Above:

View from hospital roof, Abha   *1936*

In the summer of 1936 Philby was in Abha, capital of the Asir region. He photographed these typical Abha houses with their layered walls of mudbrick and protruding stone slabs, from the roof of the hospital where he was taken by the local doctor. He counted his stay in this agreeable society "my first real taste of the Happy Arabia of the ancients".

Right:

Mecca looking west-north-west   *1936*

This view from a rooftop in Mecca, of the Great Mosque with the Ka'bah at its centre, was taken in 1936, some years after Philby's conversion to Islam. Philby was given a house in Mecca by the King in 1930 and lived in it for a few months until the court moved to Riyadh. He continued to maintain the house, and used it whenever he visited Mecca. The mosque has been completely rebuilt since this photograph was taken.

Previous pages:

Pilgrims preparing to mount for Arafat   *1936/1937*

Many of the figures in this picture are wearing pilgrim garb (ihram) with bandoliers, indicating that they form part of an escort. They are probably waiting to accompany a person of importance – perhaps King Abdul-Aziz himself. Philby converted to Islam in 1930 and made his first pilgrimage the following year. He described his feeling at fulfilling his long-held desire to become a Muslim: "The whole thing seemed strangely familiar, as if I was only doing again what I had done before."

Naja Al-Nashama pass   *1936*

This is a pass high in the rugged mountains of Asir. Two tribesmen are wrapped in warm cloaks against the cold, which can be intense in winter at this height. Philby was on his way down the Asir mountains to the border of Yemen when he took this picture in June 1936. He wrote that the sound of shepherds piping their thin tunes in the mountains reminded him of Greece.

Ruined watch-towers on the Abha road *1936*

These round watch-towers in the Asir mountains used the same combination of mudbrick
and courses of stone tiles as the houses of Abha, to ensure the mud is not washed away by
heavy rain. The tall towers used to be seen all over the mountain region of Asir.

Above:

Fortified farmhouses at Mu'fija, western end of Wadi Najran
1936

Philby travelled on to Najran in the summer of 1936. After the barren wilds of his route south from the upper end of Tathlith, the Wadi Najran looked a paradise – green, peopled, prosperous. The mudbrick houses of the region south of Abha were often built in this style, high and narrow to conserve the rich land for agriculture, and with small windows for security. The roofs could be used as terraces for relaxing and enjoying the evening breezes.

Left:

Two herding girls, Asir   *1936*

Two Asiri girls take a rest from herding goats. Straw hats of different styles, designs and brim widths, often highly decorated, were worn by herdsmen and women throughout the Asir and Tihama regions. Philby was fascinated by Asir's mountain scenery and its people, a very different Arabia from the one he knew so well. "The garden of Eden must be very like this," he wrote.

Following pages:

Procession of Fayfa tribesmen   *1936*

This photograph shows a procession of tribesmen on Jebel Fayfa, a prominent massif inland from Jizan. This is one of the most fertile areas of Saudi Arabia. Rain falls on the mountains, and wadis carry water down to the plain below. Crops such as wheat, barley and coffee are grown by farmers on the terraced hillsides.

The settlement at Qullat Al-Qutail in the mountains inland from Jizan   *1936*

This village, at about 5,000 feet, had a large number of stone-built houses clustered
together for security. Here the inhabitants enjoyed coffee and tea offered by Philby's party,
"for such luxuries appeared to be non-existent among them."

House in Jizan   *1936*

Philby reached Jizan, the port on the Tihama coast in the far south-west of Saudi Arabia,
in the winter of 1936/7 and made it his headquarters for his surveying activities along the
Saudi-Yemen border that winter. From there he made his way back to Jeddah up the coast.
This photograph shows the home of Abdul-Aziz bin Bassam, a local merchant of Jizan.
Wealthy families of the Jizan and Sabya areas built houses with this type of elaborately
decorated plasterwork.

A visit by King Abdul-Aziz to Jeddah airport in the late 1930s

The King was an enthusiastic supporter of aviation, and the arrival of aeroplanes helped to improve communications over his vast kingdom. Each year Jeddah welcomed thousands of pilgrims (now numbered in the millions), bound for Mecca. This airport was continually developed until 1981, when it was superseded by the Abdul-Aziz International Airport. Its vast Hajj terminal is projected to accommodate 15 million passengers by 2010

Jeddah airport in the late 1930s

In the late 1930s, the runway of Jeddah airport consisted of a landing ground in open desert. The airport began in 1930, when four Westland Wapiti aircraft were flown to Jeddah. The aircraft in this photograph is an Italian plane, purchased in 1936.

Above:

Inside Emir Saud's tent   *1937*

Emir Saud, later King Saud, is seen here (front left, holding a camera) in his tent where
Philby visited him in the late 1930s. At this time, Emir Saud was Viceroy of Nejd. He had
been declared Crown Prince in 1933 by his father, King Abdul-Aziz.

Right:

Yanbu harbour   *1936*

Yanbu al-Bahr, on the Red Sea coast north of Jeddah, was a significant port in ancient
times, first as a stopping point on the caravan route bringing myrrh and frankincense from
the kingdoms of South Arabia and later as a port for pilgrims arriving by sea for Medina.
Yanbu now has an industrial zone with its own harbour, which has been developed into
one of the Kingdom's foremost ports for the oil and petrochemical industries.

Bertram Thomas O.B.E.
1892-1950

Above:
Bertram Thomas in the Rub' Al-Khali, 1931.

Opposite:
Bertram Thomas' crossing of the Rub' Al-Khali, 1930-31.

Bertram Thomas was born near Bristol, and joined the Civil Service in 1908. When the First World War broke out, he served in the Somerset Light Infantry in Mesopotamia (Iraq), 1916-18. From 1925 to 1932 he was Wazir (Minister), and financial adviser to the Sultan of Muscat and Oman. In 1930, having already travelled along its fringes, he began finalising plans to cross the Rub' Al-Khali, or Empty Quarter, the vast sea of sand that stretches across the Arabian Peninsula. It was a bold plan: if he succeeded, he would be the first European ever to make the crossing.

Thomas left Muscat for Salalah in southern Oman, realising that his only protection on his journey would be the local bedouin, and that the only way to win their trust would be to accept their methods of survival; to eat what they ate, travel as they did and to share everything he had with them.

From the end of December 1930 to February 1931, Thomas and his bedouin companions traversed the dunes. He kept meticulous notes, collected specimens and recorded measurements, gathering information which he later incorporated into his classic work, Arabia Felix. He also took film footage and photographs of his journey. After 58 days of intensely hot days, freezing nights, hunger, thirst and monotony, Thomas and his 13 companions reached Doha on the shores of the Arabian Gulf. T.E. Lawrence wrote: "Bertram Thomas … has just crossed the Empty Quarter, that great desert of Southern Arabia. It remained the only unknown quarter of the world, and it is the end of the history of exploration."

Fifteen years later, Thesiger reported that he had been welcomed warmly by the bedouin of the Rub' Al-Khali because he was of the same tribe as Thomas, who had won their respect for his good nature, generosity and determination.

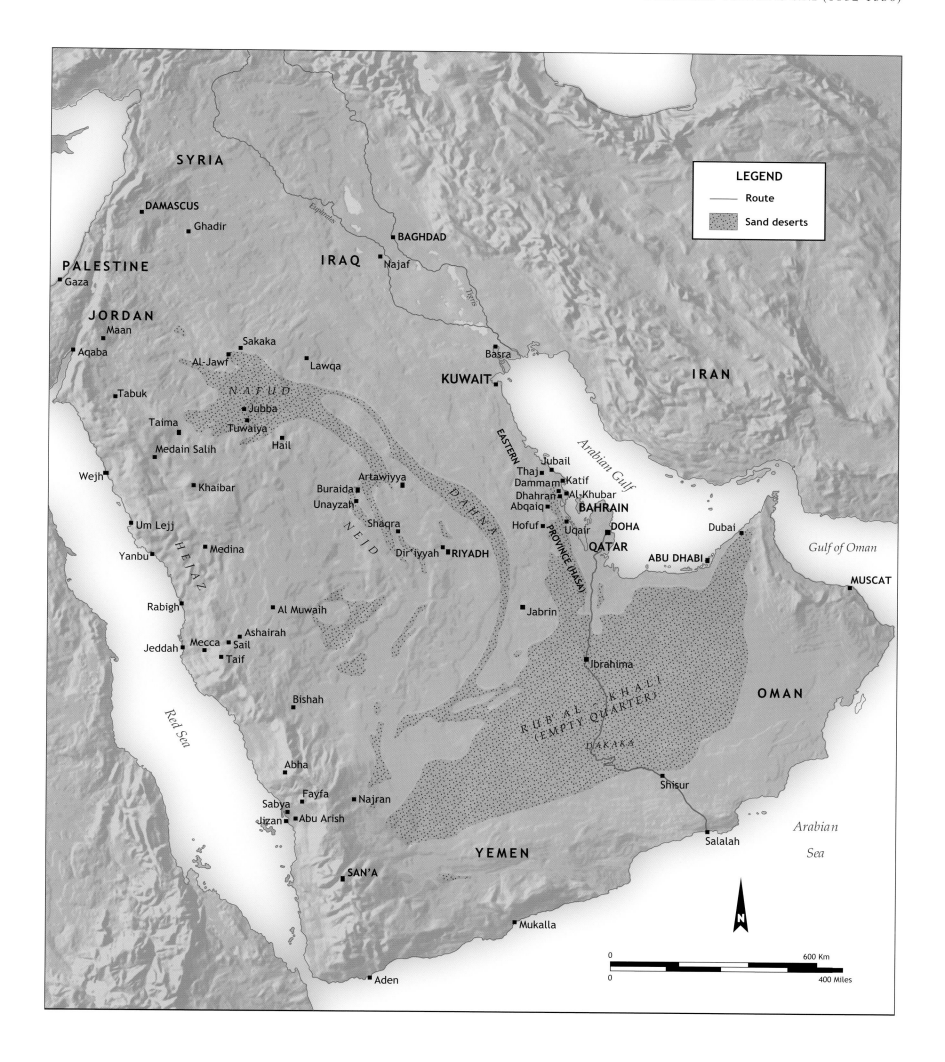

LEGEND

—— Route

Sand deserts

Marching in the mighty Uruq-adh-Dhahiya   *January 1931*

"The sands are a public diary," wrote Thomas, "that even he who runs may read, for
all living creatures go unshod. Each of my companions not only knew at a glance the
footmarks of every camel and man of my caravan, but claimed to know those of his
absent tribe, and not a few of his enemies."

A small Murra encampment, Dakaka   *January 1931*

Approaching the dunes of Dakaka, Thomas and his caravan came across this encampment
of two tents. Thomas was invited in to tend to an old man who complained of stomach
pains. "The urine of the young cow camel is taken in small quantities for such disorders,"
he reported, "or preferably her vomit (said to be less thirst-provoking)." The tents
"consisted of two 20-foot strips of very roughly woven dark brown and white wool …
every thread had been spun and woven by the women within." The leather bucket to the
right of the picture was used as a water trough.

A 'son of the sands', one of Thomas' companions on a dune near Nukhdat Fasad   *December 1930*

The long days in the desert were hungry times for Thomas and his companions, and there was precious little for the camels to eat: "So wretched was the grazing that we were obliged to split up into three parties and distribute our animals over an area of a mile or more." At night, Thomas felt the cold bitterly. "My blankets made it endurable for me … but for my companions it meant wretchedness."

Following pages:
Thomas' caravan in the central sands   *February 1931*

"In the sands themselves, man must be forever on the move," wrote Thomas. "In summer, movement is by night in sharp marches from one water-hole to another. In winter … movement is by day with a halt of perhaps two or three days; the herds move slowly across the great spaces in unending cycle."

Above:

Watering camels in the central sands   *February 1931*

Thomas was struck by the strict rules of behaviour of the bedouin in the desert. "It was their code after a thirsty day's march that when we arrived at a water-hole no drop should pass the lips of the advanced party until those in the rear had come up." He found that the code was different when it came to camels, where it was every man for himself. "This greed for their camels aroused my interest because of its strange conflict with the generosity of their personal relationships … [the camel's] welfare he seems to set above every other consideration."

Opposite above:

Typical Suwahib sands   *February 1931*

It was at this point that Thomas gave up drinking water from the wells. The water here was the colour of beer, he observed, and its brackish taste could not be disguised, even by dried soup powder. The water along this stretch proved undrinkable for his Rashidi companions too, "while in places, even their camels will turn away." Camel's milk formed Thomas' chief diet, although he often had to water it down, and it soon curdled and turned sour in his water-skins

Opposite below:

Resting in a gypsum patch   *February 1931*

Thomas observed what he described as "silver patches in the low troughs" between the sand dunes, "looking from a distance like sheets of ice or the salt residues of dried-up lakes." Such patches were in fact gypsum – in Arabic ghadera – and Thomas and his companions passed many of them on their journey north through the Rub' Al-Khali.

Gerald de Gaury M.C.
1897-1984

Above:
Gerald de Gaury in Arab dress, 1934.

Opposite:
Gerald de Gaury's trans-Arabian routes, 1934 and 1935.

While British Political Agent in Kuwait in the 1930s, Gerald de Gaury visited Riyadh several times, and left an evocative picture of the city in words and photographs.

In November 1935 he accompanied British Minister Sir Andrew Ryan on an official visit to King Abdul-Aziz. They landed at Uqair and travelled via Hofuf to Riyadh. When in Riyadh, de Gaury and Sir Andrew stayed at the Badiah guest palace, "a long, low range of castellated buildings, on the far side of the shingly-bottomed river bed [the Wadi Hanifah]." They had several meetings at the royal palace, and Sir Andrew presented the King with the Grand Cross of the Order of the Bath.

An Arabist, soldier, diplomat and historian as well as a romantic, de Gaury felt deep affection for Arabia and the Arabs. His book, Arabia Phoenix, subtitled 'An account of a visit to Ibn Saud, Chieftain of the Austere Wahabis and Powerful King of Arabia', vividly describes daily life in Riyadh in the 1930s. He was enchanted, for example, by the men who recited the Quran in the corridors, bridges and galleries of King Abdul-Aziz's palace between dusk prayers and dinner: "They sit concealed in the shadows of archways, a little distant from the king's own sitting place, so that their voices come softly to him like sustained notes on a distant organ."

In 1950, de Gaury published *Arabian Journey and Other Desert Travels*, giving an account of a wartime assignment in Nejd and Asir. During this period he spent time at the court of King Abdul-Aziz, went hunting with the royal party in the Dahna sands, and accompanied the King on the first leg of the annual Hajj. He also travelled south along the Red Sea coast to Jizan, and thence to Yemen. De Gaury continued to write on Arabian themes for much of the rest of his life.

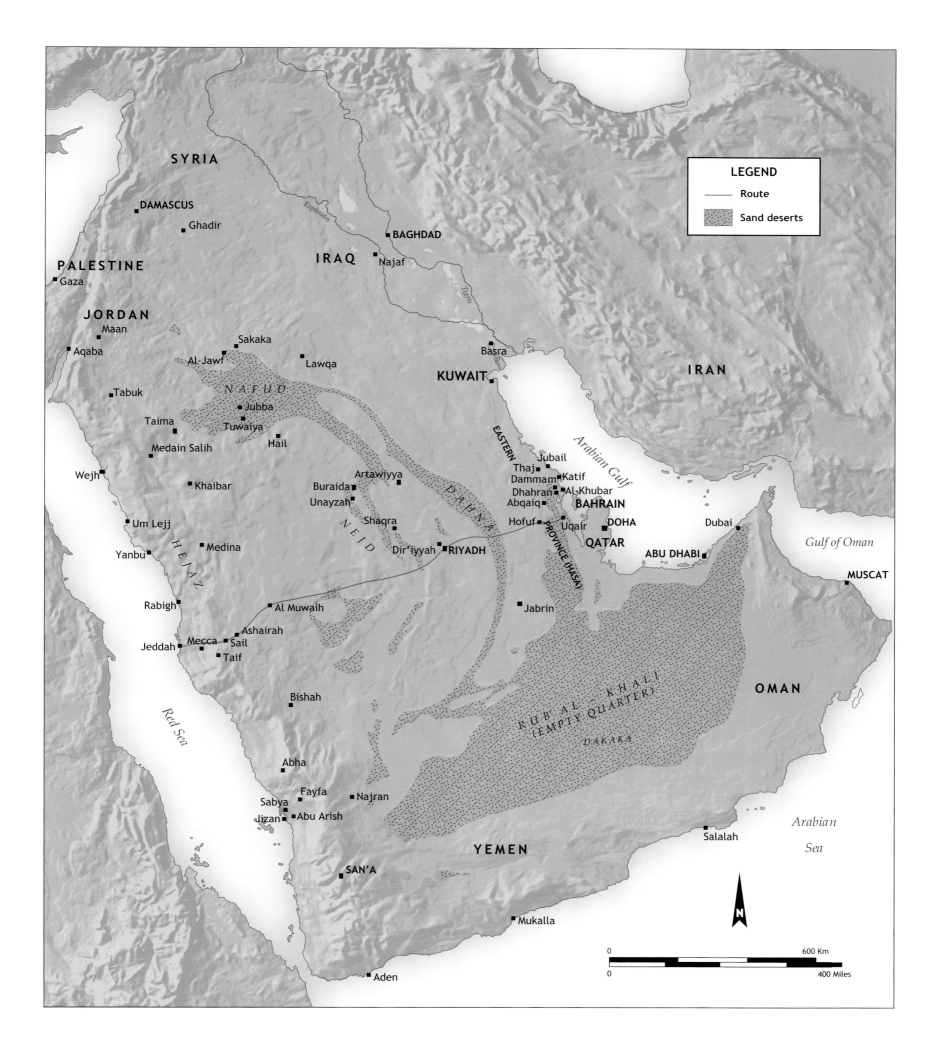

Above:

Princess Noura's house, Riyadh   *November 1935*

De Gaury arrived in Saudi Arabia at the eastern port of Uqair, and travelled by car 250 miles south-west through the Dahna sand-belts to Riyadh. One of the first buildings he saw as he approached the capital was this, the newly-built palace of the King's sister Noura. At the time, it was one of the only houses to have been built outside the city walls. Noura was the King's favourite sister; on the back of this photograph, de Gaury wrote: "when in Riyadh he [Ibn Saud] saw her every day and often consulted."

Previous pages:

King Abdul-Aziz Ibn Saud, centre, with Shaikh Ahmad al-Sabah of Kuwait (left), and Emir Saud ibn Abdul-Aziz, Crown Prince, (behind the King to the right)   *1935*

In November 1935 de Gaury travelled with British Minister Sir Andrew Ryan to Riyadh, to discuss frontier questions with the King, and to invest him with the CGB. By the time of their visit, the King was the undisputed ruler of a land which stretched from the Gulf to the Red Sea. He maintained friendly relations with the Shaikh of Kuwait, his neighbour to the north.

North-east face of Riyadh city walls and al-Jiri Gate
November 1935

De Gaury and his fellow-travellers drove "beneath the high defensive wall of Riyadh" towards their destination, the summer palace. As they drove on, "the roof-tops of the palace and the bigger houses came into view." He saw thin columns of smoke rising behind the walls, and imagined the "lavish Arabian meals being prepared in a hundred great houses."

Above:

The Murabba Palace, Riyadh   *1940*

De Gaury took this photograph of the Murabba Palace in 1940. The palace had been constructed just a few years earlier, as the primary residence of King Abdul-Aziz. The Murabba Palace was described by some as being so grand that new arrivals sometimes mistook it for the capital city itself.

Right:

Palace rooftops, Riyadh   *November 1935*

De Gaury admired the rooftops of Riyadh's palaces: "There are crenels like those at Persepolis," he wrote, "dividing slits in the wall, through which soldiers could aim their bows, while confusing the enemy as to which were heads and what was wall."

King Abdul-Aziz, Riyadh   *November 1935*

When de Gaury met the King, standing alone at the far end of a large reception room, he was very impressed. "His whole immense height was drawn up to its full … he was very still, and his cloak dropped from his shoulders to the ground in a graceful cascade of continuous line … He is well over six foot high, and robust in proportion. He is an ardent conversationalist and an indefatigable inquirer … as for his judgement and perspicacity, his men say of him that he is 'the sleuth of all sleuths on earth, swifter than the lightning in the sky'."

The Musmak Fort, Riyadh   *November 1935*

The Musmak Fort, the old citadel of Riyadh, is of great historical interest. Built during the 1860s, it was captured from the Turkish-backed Rashidi government by the young Abdul-Aziz Ibn Saud and a small raiding party in January 1902. When Abdul-Aziz began the reconstruction of Riyadh in 1911, the Musmak Fort was used as a prison. De Gaury also took a photograph of the section of the fortress door which, even today, has a spear-point from the raid embedded in its woodwork.

Prince, later King Feisal, son of King Abdul-Aziz

By the time this photograph was taken, Prince Feisal, the fourth son of King Abdul-Aziz, had already been identified as a future leader. The young man possessed many attributes required of a great ruler, attributes which can be discerned to some extent in this portrait: a presence marked by a fine bearing, inborn dignity and grace of manner. He was also a superb military leader, and a man of broad outlook. Feisal ruled over Saudi Arabia from 1964 until his death in 1975.

Palace square, Ibn Saud and Emir Saud returning after Friday prayer, Riyadh   *November 1935*

There were always crowds of people outside the main gate of the palace, and lines of guards to protect the King: "The people call him among themselves 'Ash-Shuyukh', which is the plural of shaikh," de Gaury wrote. He was struck by the number of visitors, officials and servants who crowded around the palace, especially after Friday prayer. The King, he noted, "rises before dawn to pray, and his day is divided by his religious duties."

Pilgrims arriving at Jeddah   *December 1935*

De Gaury accompanied Sir Andrew Ryan from Riyadh, through the Hejaz, to Jeddah, where all foreign diplomatic representations were then based. He was entranced by the sight of the pilgrims arriving at the dhow port of Jeddah, bound for Mecca: "The pilgrims go to Mecca at any time, to perform their Omra or intermediate pilgrimage ... until they have completed the rites they must all wear the *ihram*, pilgrim garb."

Street scene, Jeddah   *December 1935*

Tall white houses with ornately carved windows and doors, steeple-like minarets and
crooked lanes gave Jeddah a romantic, other-worldly air. De Gaury was fascinated by the
mixed origin of the people he saw on the streets. "Indians, Javanese, Africans, Chinese, and
even Bokharans and Russians, pilgrims or residents, mingle in the streets." The inhabitants
of Jeddah, he wrote, have gentle, languorous manners. "They wear cotton or silk clothes all
the year round, and their food is often cooked in foreign – Persian, Indian or Turkish –
fashion."

Sir George Rendel

1889-1979

Above:
Sir George Rendel and his wife, 1937.

Opposite:
Sir George Rendel's trans-Arabian route, 1937.

Sir George Rendel was head of the Eastern Department of the Foreign Office from 1930 to 1938. He visited Riyadh in March 1937, at the invitation of King Abdul-Aziz. Rendel and his wife landed at Uqair and travelled via Hofuf by car to Riyadh. They stayed in the newer of the two palaces at Badiah, and as a guest of the Crown Prince Emir Saud, Lady Rendel became the first European woman to be received at dinner in the royal palace. The guest palace was an attractive structure built around two columned courtyards, with much interior decoration in carved plaster and brightly painted wooden doors.

The Rendels were impressed with the city and its architecture. In the fine main square, at the end of Thumayri Street, a colonnade connected the royal palace with a guest house for tribal shaikhs. Rendel wrote, "it was a revelation to me of how fine in line and proportion modern Arabian architecture can be." King Abdul-Aziz was on pilgrimage in Mecca at the time, so Rendel had talks with the Crown Prince: "He said that the keystone of Saudi policy was friendship with Great Britain. He hoped that this guiding principle would always be maintained."

On leaving Riyadh the Rendels travelled to Jeddah on the west coast, where they spent a week. While in Jeddah, Rendel had a series of meetings with King Abdul-Aziz. "The most striking characteristic of King Ibn Saud," he wrote, "was his commanding personality. We noticed that in any group or company … he appeared at once as the outstanding figure." He concluded that, "it would have been difficult to imagine any Eastern ruler with whom it would have been more satisfactory to deal."

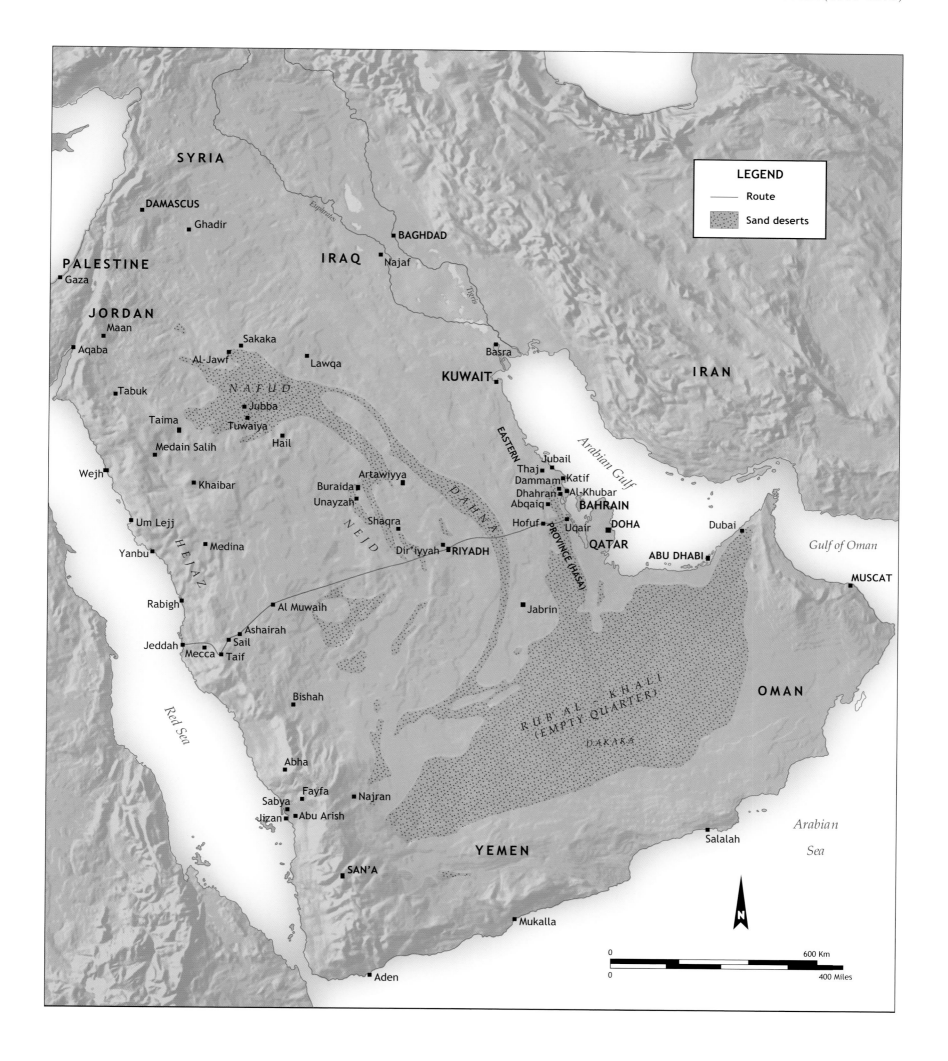

The Suq Al-Khamis, Hofuf   *1937*

This is the Suq Al-Khamis, or Thursday market, in Hofuf showing wood being sold beside
the tower of the Kut (fort). The Kut consisted of a strongly fortified enclosure with 30
bastions which formed the seat of government and the military within the main walls of
Hofuf. The Suq Al-Khamis is in the Rifa'ah quarter outside the Kut. The population of
Hofuf at the time of Rendel's visit was estimated to be around 200,000.

Previous pages:
Rendel's Chevrolet being pulled out of the sand, Hofuf

1937

Sir George and Lady Rendel drove across Arabia from Uqair to Jeddah, stopping for some
time in Riyadh en route. They made frequent halts, such as this, to drag vehicles out of the
sand. Rendel wrote: "The vast emptiness of Eastern Arabia had its own variety … every 50
miles or so we would be faced with a ten- or twenty-mile stretch of soft treacherous sand
in which many of our vehicles would get stuck."

North-eastern point of Riyadh, seen from the north, looking across the great cemetery   *1937*

The Rendels drove to Riyadh and this was the view which would have greeted them as they arrived. It is taken from the north, looking across the cemetery. Part of the old walls appear and, towering behind them, the Qasr al Musmak, or Musmak Fort. This building, which featured so significantly in the early history of the Kingdom when the future King Abdul-Aziz seized it from the occupying Rashidi garrison in 1902, still stands in the centre of the old part of Riyadh. Now restored, it is a museum dedicated to the life of King Abdul-Aziz.

Outside the palace, Riyadh   *1937*

This was King Abdul-Aziz's main palace in Riyadh, with one of the pillared viaducts which connected it to neighbouring buildings, and part of the main square in front of the palace. A palace had stood on this site since the mid-nineteenth century. Rendel described it as: "A high, fortified building with two massive towers and a simple line of perforated decoration across its great wall."

Riyadh market place   *1937*

This busy scene shows the covered stalls of Riyadh's suq, in the western part of the old
walled city. The suq was demolished in the mid-1950s to make way for a new city centre

King Abdul-Aziz in his majlis   *1937*

This photograph of King Abdul-Aziz was taken while the King was seated in his majlis or audience-chamber. The King held two audiences, one in the morning and one in the evening, during which he would hear petitions from his subjects.

A street near the palace, Riyadh *1937*

This bustling street scene was taken near the King's main palace in Riyadh. The architecture is typical of the buildings of Riyadh then: massive mudbrick walls on a stone base, relieved by triangular perforations along the walls and crenellations and rows of stepped pinnacles along the roofs. Palm-wood gutters carried rainwater from roofs into the street below. They had to project well out from the wall to ensure that overflows did not destroy the mud walls.

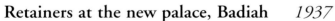

Retainers at the new palace, Badiah   *1937*

This scene is taken in one of the intricately decorated corridors of the new guest palace at Badiah, where Sir George and Lady Rendel stayed. The two Badiah palaces, which no longer exist, were used by King Abdul-Aziz as summer retreats and for guests. They stood on the Wadi Hanifah, about five miles to the west of old Riyadh, and were surrounded by orchards and date palms. The palace walls were decorated with geometric patterns and the wooden doors and shutters with painted designs, while the ceilings were covered in painted cloth and the windows hung with silk curtains.

Taif, Hejaz, descent through the granite Shafa hills *1937*

After leaving Riyadh, Sir George and Lady Rendel continued by car across Arabia to
Jeddah. En route they spent two or three days at Taif, the summer capital of the Saudi
royal family in the hills above Mecca. The picture is of a caravan of mule riders descending
through the granite Shafa hills near Taif.

115

Above:

A street in Jeddah   *1937*

Before leaving Arabia the Rendels stayed in Jeddah, at the British Legation. This picture shows the frontage of the Gellatly Hankey building, with business premises on the ground floor and staff accommodation above. The building, which was sadly demolished in the 1960s, was a fine example of Jeddah architecture. It had intricately-carved covered wooden latticed bay windows (in Arabic mashrabiyah or rawashin), which were such a feature of the older houses of Jeddah. They provided both ventilation and privacy; some still survive in the old part of the city.

Right:

Jeddah roofs   *1937*

This view was taken from the roof of the Gellatly Hankey building opposite the British Legation, looking across a corner of the British Residence over the old walled town of Jeddah, where the traditional building material was coral. Directly behind the building can be seen the minaret of the Pasha (or Basha) Mosque, while in the background is the Hanifi Mosque.

Sir Wilfred Thesiger K.B.E., D.S.O.
1910-2003

Above:
Wilfred Thesiger in the Rub' Al-Khali, 1946.

Opposite:
Wilfred Thesiger's crossings of the Rub' Al-Khali, 1946-7 and 1948.

Sir Wilfred Thesiger was born in 1910 in Addis Ababa, Ethiopia. Although he went to school and university in Britain, his early years in Africa gave him a yearning for remote places which lasted throughout his life. In 1945 Thesiger joined the Middle East Anti-Locust Unit (MEALU), and it was while working for the Unit in the Hejaz that he first experienced the powerful draw of the Empty Quarter (Rub' Al-Khali).

He crossed the Empty Quarter from south to north twice, by different routes. The first journey in 1946 started at Salalah and ended near the dunes of the Liwa Oasis. The second, in 1948, took him from Sulayyil to Abu Dhabi. Both journeys were fraught with danger from warring tribes, starvation and the uncertainty of finding the next well, but the satisfaction Thesiger derived from the silence and purity of the desert, and the companionship of his fellow travellers, is beautifully described in his masterpiece, *Arabian Sands*: "Round us was a silence in which only the winds played and a cleanness which was infinitely remote from the world of men."

In the summer of 1946 and again in 1947, Thesiger travelled the length of the Tihama coast, and back through the mountains of Asir for the MEALU. He loved Asir and was haunted by the memory of its "graceful laughing people". He described his travels there: "Sometimes we spent the night in a castle with an Emir, sometimes in a mud cabin with a slave, and everywhere we were well received."

In addition to extended stays in the Middle East and Africa, Thesiger lived in the marshes of Iraq, as reported in his well-known book *The Marsh Arabs*, and journeyed to remote areas such as the Hindu Kush and Kurdistan. But, he wrote, "none of these places has moved me as did the deserts of Arabia".

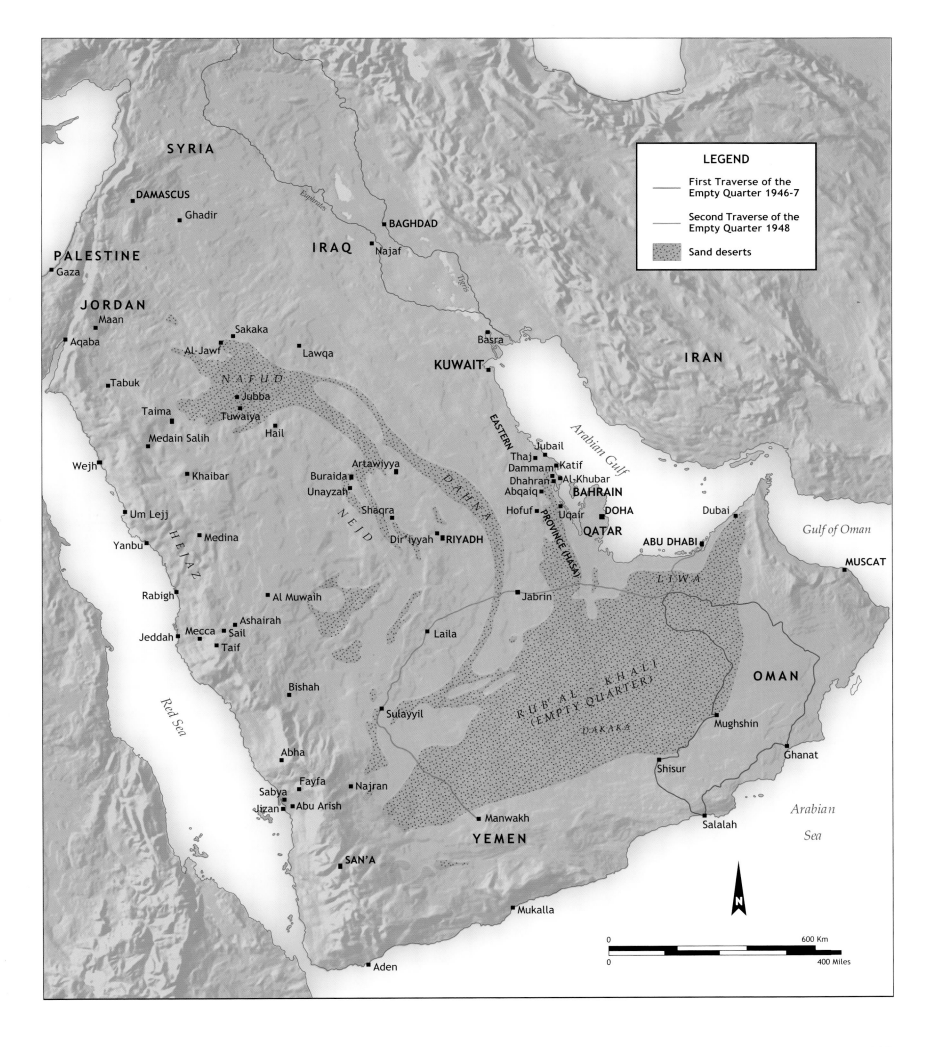

Sahul bedouin at Rumhiyya *1945*

Thesiger described the camel in Arabian Sands: "'God's gift' they call her, and it is her patience that wins the Arab's heart. I have never seen a bedu strike or ill-treat a camel. Always the camels' needs come first. It is not only that the bedu's existence depends upon the welfare of his animals, but that he has a real affection for them." Here, a group of bedouin empty their goatskin bags into a large leather trough to water the waiting camels.

Hofuf town and walls   *1946*

This is an external view of the Kut (or Qasr Ibrahim) and surrounding walls of old Hofuf.
The fort still stands but the walls have now disappeared. Hofuf lies at the south-east corner
of the great Hasa oasis, and some of the palms of this oasis can be seen near the walls of
old Hofuf. Since this picture was taken the palms have retreated, due to the exploitation of
underground water.

Spring pool, Hasa oasis *1946*

There are still underground springs forming pools in the Hasa oasis, though water levels
have dropped in recent years. The agriculture in this region was beautifully simple and
effective. It relied upon water, date palms, donkeys, cattle and alfalfa. The donkeys
provided the power for transport and water lifting, as seen in this photograph, while alfalfa
was grown as animal fodder. The animals' manure was used to fertilize the fields.

House in Zahran area, Asir   *1946*

Zahran lies north of Al-Bahah on the road to Taif. Stone-built houses of this type can still
be found here; white quartz picks out a simple decoration of straight lines and triangles. In
this area, Thesiger wrote, the people "live in massively built, single-storied houses of which
the halls are often of considerable size, their roofs supported on rows of heavy pillars of
juniper and talh [acacia] decorated with incised patterns and stained black."

Numas, tribesmen firing off their tower muskets at a circumcision dance *1946*

Numas is high in the mountains of Asir. In this part of Arabia boys and young men used to undergo circumcision as a rite of initiation. Thesiger wrote: "We arrived at Numas on the day of a circumcision ceremony ... Some 150 of the tribesmen present were armed with Tower muskets ... they surged in rapid and continuous succession into an empty threshing floor round which they rushed, throwing their muskets high in the air ... Bedecked with silver powder flasks and other trappings and dressed in their full finery, they were a brave sight seen through the eddying clouds of smoke."

Threshing in the traditional way near Abha, Asir   *1946*

A farmer, wearing one of the large-brimmed straw hats often seen in the Asir mountains even today, threshes grain with a simple plough and two hump-backed oxen. Behind him are houses typical of the construction associated with the area around Abha, chief town of Asir. Thesiger described forested mountains, ice-cold streams, wild flowers and "terraced fields of wheat and barley, vines and plots of vegetables." He reached the Abha area in May 1946 and later wrote: "In these mountains, wheat (burr) or barley (sha'ir) is sown in the winter and dhurra (sorghum) in the summer."

Shada fort, Abha   *1947*

Thesiger wrote: "Abha, a small town about 7,500 feet above sea-level, built round the
castle and having a number of shops, is an extremely important administrative centre."
The fort photographed here was built in the 1850s by the local Emir and was used later as
the headquarters of the Emirate. A section of the market can be seen below the fort.
Thesiger was enchanted by the weekly markets of Asir's towns and villages, "which sprang
up at dawn in remote valleys in the mountains or just for a day packed the streets of some
small town."

Tower houses in the Bani Malik Mountains   *1947*

Thesiger wrote: "It was delightful to travel across these cool and bracing uplands where successive villages afforded endless interest. There is variety in the construction and shape of the houses which, intended for defence, are massively built of many storeys but all have a satisfying and harmonious beauty. The guest chambers were cool and spacious, decorated around the lower walls with bands of green, red and black. Here, grouped around the coffee hearth among tribesmen on whom the discordant influence of the west had not as yet intruded, we spent long happy evenings."

On Jebel Sawdah (Suda), Asir   *1947*

Thesiger has here photographed a stone village and terraces on the slopes of Jebel Sawdah, near Abha. At over 9,000 feet, it is the highest point in Arabia. Jebel Sawdah receives more rainfall than any other part of the Asir region and, as a result, olives, prickly pears, aloes, juniper and many other shrubs and flowering plants bloom luxuriantly. Its slopes have now been conserved as a national park.

Crushing sesame seeds at Sabya   *1947*

In 1947 Thesiger followed his 1945 route down the coast from Jeddah to Jizan via Sabya. He described Sabya as "a large town of grass huts with a few stone buildings". Sesame seed oil was one of the main products of coastal Tihama; the oil was milled by the patient circumambulation of a blinkered camel. In the background of this photograph are ushash, the conical brushwood and mud dwellings typical of the Tihama.

Following pages:
Ushash at Abu Arish in the Tihama   *1947*

Abu Arish lies inland from Jizan at the southern end of the Tihama. Thesiger here records two splendid examples of Tihama houses which the local people called ushash, meaning 'nests'. They were built of brushwood and daub, with conical or rectangular roofs of brushwood thatch, all held together with plaits of rope. The interiors of these houses were plastered with clay, and brightly painted.

Photographic Credits:

Every effort has been made to contact owners of copyright material.
The following photographers and institutions are gratefully acknowledged for their contributions:

The British Library: 10
Imperial War Museum: 36, 38, 39, 40, 41, 42-43, 44*t*, 44-45
National Portrait Gallery: 2, 6,
Pitt Rivers Museum, University of Oxford: 118, 120, 121, 122, 123, 124, 125, 126, 127, 128, 129, 130-131
Royal Geographical Society: 16, 18-19, 20, 21, 22-23, 24-25, 26-27, 30, 31, 32-33, 46, 47, 48, 49, 50-51, 52, 53, 54-55, 57*t*, 57*b*, 58-59, 60, 61, 62, 64-65, 66*t*, 66-67, 68, 69, 70-71, 71*t*, 72-73, 74, 75, 76, 77, 78*t*, 78-79, 80, 82, 83, 84-85, 86-87, 88, 89*t*, 89*b*, 90, 92-93, 94, 95, 96*t*, 96-97, 98, 99, 100, 100-101, 102, 103, 104, 106-107, 108, 109, 110, 111, 112, 113, 114, 114-115, 116*t*, 116-117
University of Newcastle upon Tyne, Gertrude Bell Photographic Archive: 28, 34, 35
The Wentworth Collection, The British Library: 12, 13, 14, 15